More Praise for *Rapid Media Development for Trainers*

"If you're a training professional who uses any type of media (video, audio, graphics, or screen text) in your learning programs, then *Rapid Media Development for Trainers* is for you. Jonathan Halls draws upon his 25-plus years of experience in media development and learning psychology to explain these topics in simple terms. He explains why media development is important, and how it fits into the context of learning. He shares well-researched insight into media design, as well as lessons learned from his own vast experience, and equips you with proven techniques to use when creating your own projects. You'll reach for this reference guide again and again when designing or delivering training programs. I can't wait to add this new book to my resource collection!"

—Cindy Huggett
Author, *The Virtual Training Guidebook:
How to Design, Deliver, and Implement Live Online Learning*

"Whether you're a classroom trainer or an e-learning developer, *Rapid Media Development for Trainers* is a great primer on incorporating digital media into your toolkit. From capturing and editing audio, to creating guerilla-style or more formal video assets, to incorporating graphics and onscreen text, Jonathan Halls digs into virtually every aspect of digital media creation."

—Cammy Bean
Author, *The Accidental Instructional Designer:
Learning Design for the Digital Age*

"Being media-development-savvy might have once been a specialty or luxury in the learning space, but it is fast becoming the norm—at least in the minds of today's and tomorrow's learners. For learning professionals, understanding and being adept at designing and developing digital content is what will soon separate the 'indispensable' from the 'passé.' In *Rapid Media Development for Trainers*, Jonathan Halls has created a must-have guide to help you bridge this skill gap and get your media development game on point!"

—Halelly Azulay
Author, *Employee Development on a Shoestring*
Host, *The TalentGrow Show* Leadership Podcast
Leadership Development Strategist at TalentGrow

D1597430

Rapid Media Development for Trainers

Creating Videos, Podcasts, and
Presentations on a Budget

JONATHAN HALLS

PRESS

Cover Imagery: Thinkstock
Photographs on pages 16, 100, and 120-127 by John Body. All other photographs, and
Figures 14-1 and 14-2, by Shutterstock.
TechSmith product screenshot(s) reprinted with permission from TechSmith Corporation.
Audacity® software is copyright © 1999-2016 Audacity Team. The name Audacity® is a
registered trademark of Dominic Mazzoni.

ATD Press is an internationally renowned source of insightful and practical information on
talent development, workplace learning, and professional development.

ATD Press
1640 King Street
Alexandria, VA 22314 USA

Ordering information: Books published by ATD Press can be purchased by visiting ATD's
website at www.td.org/books or by calling 800.628.2783 or 703.683.8100.

Library of Congress Control Number: 2016957825
ISBN-10: 1-56286-585-4
ISBN-13: 978-1-56286-585-6
e-ISBN: 978-1-56286-586-3

ATD Press Editorial Staff
Director: Kristine Luecker
Manager: Christian Green
Community of Practice Manager, Learning Technologies: Justin Brusino
Developmental Editor: Jack Harlow
Associate Editor: Caroline Coppel
Cover Design: Charles Brock, Faceout Studio
Text Design: Maggie Hyde and Iris Sanchez
Printed by Versa Press, Inc., East Peoria, IL

Contents

Preface

It's a noble endeavor to be a learning professional. When people allow you to influence their thinking, it's a privilege beyond words. We as a community of professionals should never take this for granted. A hundred years ago, this privilege lived mostly in classrooms. In the 1930s, radio gave our profession a new venue. Soon after that, television. Now, the 21st century offers many more spaces for learners to build knowledge and skills. We face new modalities, new platforms, new calls for personalization.

Our influence truly extends beyond the classroom. And just as we need skills to deliver meaningful learning in the classroom, learning professionals need solid skills and disciplined methods if we are to influence learners in these new spaces. The skills of classroom facilitation take time to learn, as well as a lifetime of successes and failures to perfect; it is no different with media production. It is just as unconscionable to leave it to chance when developing media as it is when preparing for the classroom. You might be able to get by once or twice, but there's a real discipline to consistently producing quality media. Above all, winging it mocks the privilege learners have given us to influence them.

We need to be disciplined and skillful with media content. This can seem daunting for many learning professionals with limited experience recording a podcast, shooting a video, designing a graphic, or writing screen text. So when Justin Brusino, who talked me into writing my first book, suggested grabbing a beer to talk about another, I threw out the idea of drawing together these modalities into one book. There are some great books that focus on individual modalities such as video, audio, graphics, and screen text. But learning professionals are more and more being asked to work with all of them, and so I have written this book for readers who want to become masters at creating learning media.

In a way this book reflects some of the workshops I have done over the past decade and a half in London, Singapore, and Washington, D.C., on concepts relating to 360-degree storytelling and transmedia. After all, in the future we'll need to use different modalities and platforms interchangeably, blended with other learning methodologies. Thankfully, Justin bought the idea and the beer, and has once again patiently guided me through the proposal process. Thanks, Justin.

I've sought to do two things in this book. First, to distill what I've learned over the past 25 years into a foundational framework that offers a mindset for thinking about constructing content that will cause learning. Second, to share practical methods, drawn from the professional media world and applied to consumer-level equipment, that will help you consistently make high-quality media content.

This book attempts to provide breadth rather than depth. It's tough to squeeze 25 years of experience and learning into a couple hundred pages. So I have aimed to provide this framework as a tool you can use to deepen your skills and knowledge with practice and experience. It's been tough to write because, like any subject matter expert, I've been tempted every step of the way to cram in more details, rather than remain focused on providing a foundation. It's the subject matter expert's curse. But Jack Harlow, my development editor, has helped me stay disciplined and keep this book foundational. Thanks, Jack.

Thanks also to Associate Editor Caroline Coppel, who oversaw the copy edits and shepherded me through the production of the book and subsequent reviews. She has been patient and understanding, which I have especially appreciated because she has worked around my relentless schedule of seminars and travel.

I know a lot about learning psychology and its relation to audio, video, and writing. I've been studying and teaching it for years. But I'm a "layman with an opinion" when it comes to graphics, not an expert. And yet it's one of the modalities we all use, whether it be for presentation slides, in handouts, or part of a e-learning program. So I faced the challenge of whether to research and write as a journalist or consult a recognized expert. After a conversation with Justin and Jack, I thought, why not ask Connie Malamed to write a chapter? Connie comes to graphics with a healthy balance of being both a graphics expert and instructional design guru. And she's a great writer. Her book *Visual Language for Designers* is both an instructive and visually beautiful book, informed by cognitive principles. As with her other books, it belongs on your shelf if you're serious about media. I am so pleased that she agreed, and I am hugely grateful for her writing chapter 14.

I am very conscious that what I write is as much about what I have learned from others as it is about my own thinking. So it's fair to say that this book reflects the wisdom and skills of many people who have taken me under their wing. During my earliest days of broadcasting, the late Alex Vale and Bruce McNeily were both hugely influential. Later, my days at BBC Production Training were incredible. While I had the honor to be a steward of this prestigious organization, the wisdom, expertise, wit, and good nature of its faculty shaped my thinking. This especially includes former colleagues at the Elstree and New Media training units in London: Paul Myers, Phil Ross, Simon Fox, Ian Hider, Paul Roberts, Simon Kidd, Mike Wright, Gareth Watkins, Ian Wyatt, Nigel Maslin, and others who were all my teachers. This book is as much yours as mine.

I also want to thank the participants of my workshops around the world with whom I have worked. Literally thousands of people in more than 25 countries have shaped my thinking with tough questions and thoughtful challenges. And their ensuing content production has been truly inspiring.

Writing can be a lonely pursuit. You withdraw from people to think, plan, write, and then rewrite. And then rewrite again. You stop answering emails and find yourself distracted when hanging out with friends as your mind continues to wander back to elements of the book you are struggling with. But it's not all that lonely when you have the support of someone special. My wife, Sharon, is that special person, always an enormous support. She stayed up late on our vacation helping me scour the manuscript for typos and providing comments. And she put up with my absentmindedness and blank stares for weeks at a time during the writing period. This book is as much her success as it is mine.

Again, it's a noble endeavor to be a learning professional. The fact that people open their minds and allow us to influence them, whether it be in a classroom or through a podcast they enjoy on their phone, is an incredible privilege. It's the same with books. I'm privileged that you picked up this one and genuinely hope its influence provides a foundation for you to become a master at creating rapid media content for learning.

Jonathan Halls
Washington, D.C.
December 2016

The New Learning Frontier: Digital Content

In This Chapter:
- What skills do learning professionals, whether they are trainers, teachers, or professors, need to create digital learning content?
- What are the three characteristics of the new digital content ecosystem?

Learning professionals have always worked with media. Whether it's a flipchart, mimeographed handouts, or acetates on an overhead projector, media has always been an important part of delivering training and educating people. It provides learners with multiple ways of learning and reinforcement. For example, an acetate shown on an overhead projector can more efficiently illustrate how a car works than just a trainer's verbal description. And providing handouts gives learners something concrete they can refer to after the learning event.

Until about 10 years ago, media such as audio or video was produced by broadcast professionals who had big budgets and advanced technical skills. They used expensive, complicated cameras and fancy microphones and tape recorders, and generally worked in TV and radio stations or production houses. The equipment simply was not accessible to the average trainer, and even had it been, it was very complicated to learn and use.

But that's all changed. Today, you can create your own audio and video content for use in the physical classroom and virtual learning ecosystem for a fraction of what it would cost to hire a production team. And using media is no longer a matter of owning one VHS copy of a sales training video that you guard jealously and never loan out in case it's not returned. Today, you can create your own audio, video, graphics, and screen text content that the learner can access any way she wants—on a phone, tablet, or desktop. She can access it anywhere that has an Internet connection and anytime that suits her schedule.

If you've attended a conference anytime over the past decade, you'll have heard people using buzzwords like *blended learning*, *flipped classroom*, *MOOCs*, *augmented reality*, and *social learning*. In fact, you may already be exploring these new approaches to learning in your own work. Given that these innovations are becoming common words in the learning professional's lexicon, it's easy to become blasé and forget how profound they are—and to miss the profundity of the changes likely to come down the pike in the future. This is probably because our world is change-weary.

The amount and speed of change for most people probably became most apparent about 15 years ago, when a connection to the Internet became common for many people in the workplace. The innovations since then have been dizzying.

What Is Media?

A lot of people think of *media* as a collective term for radio, television, and newspapers. *Media* comes from the word *medium*, which means an intervening agency, means, or instrument by which something is conveyed. TV, radio, and newspapers convey information. But so do many other things. A signpost on the side of the road is a medium, as is a bumper sticker or a restaurant menu. Learning professionals have used many media over the years, including chalkboards, films shown on movie projectors, slides, felt displays, and even posters. In this book, the term *media* is used in its broadest term as anything that is a means to convey information.

Flashback

Let's reflect on what this change has been. In the mid- to late 1990s, the Internet was that thing on a computer in the corner of the office or a library. In some workplaces, you had to book time to use it. A few years later the Internet knocked on our front doors in the form of the old dial-up modem that coughed and spluttered to bring us content from the world's big providers, like AOL, BBC, and AltaVista. It most often took 30 to 40 seconds for a page to download. This was less than 20 years ago.

The Internet became more reliable a few years later, with broadband connections using the existing copper cable technologies that had supported telephones. Then fiber optic burst on the scene, offering scorching fast bandwidth speeds. Now the Internet travels in your pocket and briefcase through your smartphone and tablet.

The first webpages were mostly made up of the written word, although some included images that took forever to download. Then, developers introduced audio to the web, such as Real Networks, which developed RealAudio Player in the mid-1990s. Video then became a reality, boosted by YouTube, formed in 2005.

It's incredible to think about how much has changed in the past few decades and compare it with the changes in communication through history. Take for example the printing press, which radically changed society. It took half a millennia to innovate the next communication technology, the telegraph. And it's not just the technology that has changed, but also our lifestyles. In the United States, there are more mobile phones than people. According to a 2013 report from IDC, 79 percent of smartphone users reach for their device within 15 minutes of waking, showing the role these devices play in today's lifestyle. More recent research by Gallup shows that the majority of smartphone users check their phone at least once every hour. Half check their phones several times an hour (Newport 2015). People are connected and using the new technologies in so many ways that learning professionals have incredible opportunities not available before to help their learners develop new skills.

In the span of time equal to half the average person's career, the amount of change has exploded, and there's no sign it will stop. For learning professionals, the media tools we can add to our professional toolkit have expanded dramatically. This new range of tools offers more flexibility for the learner and greater precision in delivering content. Now any trainer, teacher, or professor can create audio podcasts or videos, publish online content, and design graphics to help their learners. But of course just being able to make content does not mean the content is good or will actually lead to learning. The challenge for learning professionals is to take it from being just a new form of media to something that is professional and deliberately structured to lead to learning.

Purpose of This Book

Written for learning professionals, *Rapid Media Development for Trainers* will help you make polished digital content that aids learning. It's easy to think that the principles and techniques we explore are relevant for stand-alone content, such as videos you may show in the classroom or podcasts you make available on demand through a learning management system. However, they are also relevant for building PowerPoint presentations that form the basis for e-learning content. The disciplined, creative use of digital content such as audio and video can add life to what might otherwise be dull e-learning experiences.

The focus is on the four modalities most within learning professionals' reach:

- video
- audio
- graphics
- screen text.

These modalities will be explored in the context of two important characteristics of digital content: multiplatform distribution and personalization.

One challenge of the topic of digital content is that many people instinctively put this book on the shelf with their books about learning technologies. While this book talks about technology, it is not a technology book. It doesn't get into the intricacies of HTML, JavaScript, or audio and video codecs, all of which will continue to change in the future. There will be no ogling over cameras or discussions about whether Adobe Premiere is better than Apple Final Cut. It's actually about learning and how these new everyday tools can help you in the noble practice of helping others learn. As such, this book is about the psychologies of learning and media, the art and science of teaching, and the practice of production.

Throughout this book, we will use the term *learning professional*. While there are significant differences among workplaces, schools, and colleges, the actual cognitive process of learning is the same for adults and children. More research from both the adult learning and K-12 learning worlds is being drawn on by respective practitioners. For example, you'll see in chapter 2 that Atkinson and Shiffrin's memory process model is used to explain learning and media communication. Their model is used by special education teachers in schools as well as trainers working in the field of skills development and expertise. It's also referenced in media psychology. So this book is written for anyone engaged in the business of helping other people learn, whether they are workplace trainers, teachers, or professors.

Essential Digital Media Skills for Learning Professionals

We're at a point when media competencies will soon become an important part of the learning professional's job description. Right now, many learning professionals are exploring how to incorporate digital content into curriculums to make learning more dynamic. They are engaging in exciting innovation.

However, if you review their work you'll be surprised at how much is dull, uninspiring, and boring. And how much really looks amateur. This is only natural: The typical learning professional didn't go to film school or study to work in broadcast radio. They went to college and mostly learned how to facilitate learning in a classroom. But the ability to create professional-looking media soon will be the baseline standard. Video shot with a wobbly camera won't be acceptable. Podcasts that have poor audio quality or fail to engage the listener won't be acceptable. Graphics designed with no purpose or meaning won't be acceptable. Screen text organized haphazardly or amateurishly crafted won't be acceptable.

Learning professionals need a deliberate set of skills that draws together both teaching and media competencies. One without the other will not be enough. Just about every trainer or teacher has heard comments like "I'm a good talker, so I can easily deliver a great training session" or "I'm a subject matter expert, so I'm perfect for designing this class." Such statements betray a fundamental misunderstanding of what skills are required to successfully manage the classroom dynamic and create experiences that lead to learning. They exude an ignorance of the instructional design processes that make complex information easy to learn. And they demonstrate an incomprehension of the practical skills, based on research into the science of learning, that are required to successfully facilitate learning and take years to refine.

Such flippancy is not that much different from saying "I'm good with technology, so I can easily shoot video and create digital learning content" or "I'm good with software, so I can edit the audio into a podcast." These statements also undervalue all that goes into crafting truly engaging and inspiring content. To that end, as our profession learns what digital content competencies for learning professionals look like, this book hopes to inform that conversation in a practical way by drawing together media and learning psychologies and mapping them to the practical production techniques and standards used in today's media world.

The Digital Content Ecosystem

To make sense of how digital content can transform your learning practice, it's helpful to consider the digital content ecosystem. Let's start by reviewing the general media world and other aspects beyond the learning world. Most people are exposed daily to the world of digital content. They're reading online newspapers and magazines, posting messages on Facebook, watching videos on YouTube, sending emails, and conducting web searches. However, in our chaotic lives it can be hard to find time to reflect on how these things piece together. There are numerous ways to dissect it, but this book will consider three important characteristics of the new digital content ecosystem and then consider what they mean for learning. They are:

- Digital content is multimodal.
- Digital content is multiplatform.
- Digital content can be personalized.

The main focus of this book is on the multimodal aspect of digital content. However, you will also benefit from an understanding of digital content within the context of multiple platforms and personalization.

What Is Digital Content?

The term *digital content* is mostly used to refer to digital media such as text, graphics, audio, and video. However, technically speaking, it is information or data that have been coded as binary digits: Think ones and zeros. So digital content can also include software and information such as GPS coordinates. This book adopts the more general use of the term and uses it to describe text, graphics, audio, and video that is published electronically or made available for download on multiple platforms and that offers an opportunity for the end user to personalize it.

The idea of multimodal content revolves around the word *convergence*. Convergence is a buzzword that's been around for a long time and refers to the coming together of technologies. The web is classic convergence because it brings together the computer, telephone, television, radio, and newspaper to one device or platform. Twenty years ago you had to go buy a newspaper to read the *New York Times'* editorial on the presidential primaries. Then you had to go into your den and turn on the TV to see what the candidate looked like kissing babies and shaking hands. To hear a discussion that goes into more depth, you might listen to the radio in your car. The physical experiences we had with audio, video, and the written word were generally very separate because they were different self-contained media that relied on different modes of communication. TV was driven by pictures and generally struggled to efficiently convey detailed content that was not visual. Radio used the spoken word, which afforded it more detail but struggled to convey facts and figures. Newspapers provided a more sit-down and in-depth experience, which allowed for details and analysis. In addition to the different modes of communication, people tended to consume text, audio, and video at separate times in the day: newspaper in the morning, radio during commutes to and from work, and TV in the evening.

All of this changed with convergence—the coming together of technology. Computers and telephones, particularly today's smartphones, brought the convergence of audio, video, text, and graphics modalities. This means you can read the editorial on the *New York Times'* webpage and move your mouse or finger and click on a video or podcast to create a seamless, multimodal experience. Convergence has also altered the physiological experience of media consumption. We no longer move to a room that has a television to see video, or head outside for the morning's copy of the *Wall Street Journal* tossed on the doorstep by a kid delivering newspapers. Everything is now on one device. And that device travels with us. You no longer go to the medium for the content; the content comes directly to you.

Following convergence, digital content has also experienced a divergence. The web—which for many people was an entity residing on a desktop computer—has effectively diverged to other platforms, so it exists now on smartphones, tablets, and other seemingly unrelated objects like cars, game consoles, home alarms, and even weather devices. The web will continue to connect more and more devices.

It's important to stay abreast of these developments because what's described here is just the start. The opportunity to give more control to learners through digital technology will continue to gather pace. Experts already predict with certainty that physical connectivity will extend to robots and even neural implants. Yes, that's right: Advanced research is under way to use neural implants to treat and manage neurological conditions such as post–traumatic stress disorder. How long will it be before such technology is able to plug into a brain much like a USB stick and provide the knowledge and skills to perform a psychomotor skill?

New technologies now allow content producers of any type to create a personalized experience for the individual recipient. For example, Amazon remembers what you have previously bought and browsed to build a profile of your interests. It suggests other products it thinks you might like. Your shopfront is personalized to your tastes so the Amazon homepage you see on your tablet, as you wait for a flight at the airport, is very different from what the person sitting next to you sees on his Amazon homepage.

Let's dig a little deeper into what this means for learning professionals.

The Web vs. the Internet

The terms *World Wide Web* and *Internet* are often used interchangeably. However, they are different. The Internet is the system of physical connections of billions of computer networks and devices around the world. It has been around since the 1960s. Applications like the web, email, Voice over Internet Protocol (VoIP), and file sharing use the Internet.

The web is a system of content that is viewed using a web browser such as Explorer or Safari. It is made up of webpages containing text, graphics, video, and audio files. Each page has its own name or address called a URL. These pages contain hyperlinks, the driver of interactivity, which connect to other digital content. The web was invented in 1989 by British scientist Tim Berners-Lee. The web is often called a medium, and although this is a helpful analogy, it is probably more accurate to call it a space where information resides.

Digital Content Is Multimodal

Your digital learning content could be experienced through multiple modalities.

For example, if you are teaching a mechanic to change a car tire, you might choose video because it involves psychomotor skills. Or if you are teaching a salesperson how to sell a new product, you might use a combination of these modalities, such as a webpage that seamlessly blends video, graphics, and screen text.

Each modality has its own set of strengths and weaknesses for communicating information and stories. It's up to you to choose the modality that best fits the topic of learning. You wouldn't start by picking the modality—say, video—and then searching for content that would be well suited for it. Instead, the digital learning professional looks at the learning objective first and then asks, "What is the best modality in which to present this objective?" We'll dive deeper throughout the book when we work through the editorial and production issues of each modality. But first, let's spend a few moments exploring each one:

- **Video:** Video is perfect for showing action, space, and to a lesser extent, interesting visual content. It can communicate action faster than words and more realistically than graphics. However, it struggles to convey complex, detailed information, and if there's no action, viewers very quickly get bored.

- **Audio:** Audio is good for narrative learning and has been described as the "theater of the mind" because it forces the listener to draw on her imagination and memory to construct meaning. It uses music and sound effects as well as the spoken word; because of this, it can be a powerful modality. However, audio struggles to convey complex information with lots of detail, and learners must listen from beginning to end to get a sense of the overall message, which may be time-consuming.

- **Images:** Graphics and photographs are good for quickly communicating information such as relationships, space, and emotions. They also bring an aesthetic quality and are helpful when communicating to groups that speak more than one language. Images are also easier to remember. But graphics work best when they focus on single points of information and may struggle to convey lengthy ranges of information. They also are not as effective for conveying concrete, specific information, such as quotations or legal messages. For example, if you use a picture of someone smiling, is that smile happy or sarcastic?

- **Screen Text:** The written word is good for conveying concrete, specific information such as facts, figures, and complex ideas. It is ideal for concise, detailed knowledge. However, it is not always the fastest way to communicate, and it can struggle to convey some abstract concepts that may be better expressed with graphical diagrams. For example, a diagram may be more effective than two pages of text at showing how a car engine works.

Multimodal Versus Multimedia

This book uses the term *multimodal* rather than the more popular *multimedia*. Multimodal is more descriptive for our purpose because audio, video, text, and images are not the physical medium, rather they are modes of communication that exist in a space that is consumed through a medium such as a tablet or smartphone.

Other Forms of Content

If you're creating educational content, you may be involved in other forms that are closely linked to these four modalities. However, the cost and level of complexity to produce them makes it likely that you would outsource their production. While the average learning professional can most likely find time to learn and make videos, podcasts, and presentations, the following content forms pretty much require full-time attention from highly skilled craftspeople.

- **Video Animation:** This could be a technical diagram that sequentially shows what happens when an airline passenger goes through each step of screening at an airport. Or it could also be a cartoonlike video. Animation is complex and requires training to pull off well.

- **Augmented Reality:** This is when information is overlaid on a live picture. For example, in a historic house such as Thomas Jefferson's Monticello, tourists walking through his office might aim their smartphone at his desk, which contains a writing polygraph (a clever device that duplicated his handwriting), and either text or a graphical overlay would explain the machine or the fact he wrote more than 20,000 letters using it. Then, if the tourists turned the phone's camera down the corridor to the library, they might see a description of the library and interesting information, such as the fact that Jefferson had owned 6,000 books that were ultimately donated to the Library of Congress. Augmented reality seems somewhat futuristic, but it's already in use.
- **Data Stories:** This is something more common in newspapers and mainstream media. A graphical interface is created to tell an evolving story, when changes can easily be tracked by data. For example, it might be a map of U.S. electoral districts showing voting patterns or the actual results of a live election. Or it may be something that changes more gradually, such as demographic or GDP information for different countries, which changes annually. The data might be input manually or automatically.

Digital Content Is Multiplatform

Digital content no longer exists on just one device, with learners logging in to their work or personal desktop to access learning material. Today, people access learning on smartphones, tablets, laptops, and desktop computers. Because digital content has become multiplatform, here are three things to consider when producing learning material:

1. the physical relationship between the learner and device
2. the importance of identifying which platform is best for the learner
3. the practical considerations of making content for multiple platforms.

The Physical Relationship

The physical relationship the learner has with a device is critical and affects his pace of learning as well as motivation. Consider how video is experienced across different platforms. When you watch video on an IMAX screen, the picture is enormous and you literally move your head from left to right to experience the film. It's incredibly immersive; the lights are turned out, which reduces distractions, and the soundtrack is produced in surround sound to make the whole experience very realistic.

Watching at home on your television is entirely different. The television is likely set up on the other side of the room, maybe 10 to 15 feet away from you. Unlike watching at the cinema, you will move your eyes to take everything in. You might be in the kitchen or otherwise distracted, and the acoustics are unlikely to be as good as in the cinema. The experience is much less immersive.

Consider watching that same video on your computer. Neither your head nor eyes move because the screen is only a foot or so away. And there's every chance you'll be interrupted by email and the temptation to check the web for something. It's even less immersive than watching TV.

That same video will be much different on your smartphone. Rather than moving your eyes, you'll move your hand toward your eyes as you bring the screen closer to you. The panoramic shots that were awesome at the cinema look tiny and crunched on your phone. But it's cool because you can take the content with you.

The same video, experienced on different devices, looks incredibly different. And the experience is different too. What does this mean for learning?

What's Best for the Learner?

Depending on who your learner is, different platforms will be more appropriate. If your learner is office-based, producing content for desktops may be most appropriate. If you're providing just-in-time learning for mechanics or technicians who visit client sites to fix things, content on a mobile device, either a smartphone or tablet, might work best.

In the future, content will be delivered on more than just desktops, smartphones, and tablets, and learning professionals need to keep up-to-date with these new innovations. *Internet of Things* is a term used to describe how physical objects become part of the Internet by having sensors, electronics, and software embedded that connect to other objects and software to exchange real-time data that can be used for all manner of tasks. Buildings already connect to the Internet to provide security, and cars use it for maps and live traffic updates. Our challenge will be learning how to make our content work for those emerging platforms.

Practical Considerations

Creating content for different platforms can get messy because not all objects are the same. Computer screens are generally bigger than tablets, so content will look different on each device. And even individual models will improve with future releases.

For example, 15 years ago the average webpage was designed to have a resolution of 800 x 600 pixels. As screen quality improved, designers started designing for 1024 x 768 pixels. When smartphones offered web connectivity, people were viewing web pages designed for 1024 x 768 pixels on phones with much smaller screens. Phones are catching up, but even now there are significant differences. The Apple iPhone 7, for example, is 1334 x 750 pixels, and the Samsung Galaxy S7 has a resolution of 2650 x 1440. And just to keep us on our feet, tablets feature a whole range of different dimensions.

But remembering exact dimensions is not the point, partly because they'll continue to change. More important is that every device is different and if we design digital content for one screen it's going to look odd on all the others. So this presents challenges. Do we create a special version of our content for each platform or device model? Or do we create one that matches the lowest common denominator? Or do we look for something that can morph into the appropriate size for different devices?

In their book, *Mobile Usability*, Jakob Nielsen and Raluca Budiu (2013) argue persuasively that content should be made specifically for each platform to take advantage of the user experience it offers. This means considering the pros and cons for each platform. For example, accessing content on a smartphone offers portability and on-demand access to learning. However, navigating with a finger, rather than with a mouse, is much clumsier. So interfaces need to be designed taking this into account. Likewise, content needs to be designed differently. Video that looks great on the big screen or on television can look unnatural on a mobile device and movement such as pans or zooms might jerk abruptly.

While Nielsen and Budiu are referencing general content in their book, as opposed to sites specifically for learning, they suggest you should have a specific site for desktop, another site or app for phones, and another for tablets. This gets expensive. An alternative is to adopt what's known as responsive design, which optimizes your website to display differently on different devices, taking into consideration their screen resolution.

Digital Content Is Personalized

The third characteristic of digital content is that it is personalized. Apart from the very personal experience of carrying content around on your tablet or phone, technology allows producers to offer content that can intuitively meet specific needs while also giving users the opportunity to tailor content. Earlier, we discussed websites like Amazon that suggest books or products you might consider purchasing based on what you previously bought or products you browsed. While Amazon offers personalized suggestions, other platforms, such as Spotify and Pandora for music, give users control over personalization. You can choose your favorite genre or songs and create a virtual radio station that plays the music you like, ignoring what you don't, wresting control from the radio station's music director and firmly giving it to the user.

Learning professionals know that being able to personalize learning deepens the experience and offers greater autonomy, leading to more ownership of the learning experience. Technology allows us to make our content even more learner centered. What does this look like in more practical terms?

- **Content is available on demand:** Learners can learn when it suits their schedules, preferences, and needs. If it's a formal course of study, they can plan learning around their work. If it's short chunks of learning, such as nano- or microlearning, it can be available when the person needs it, just in time.
- **Content is nonlinear:** Learners can take modules of a course of learning in any order they want. If they want to start with theory before practice, they can do that. The other

way round is fine too—it's their choice. Of course, some curriculums need to follow a sequential progression, but quite a few do not. In addition, some learners may come with prior knowledge and would want to skip the more basic modules.

- **Authorship is shared:** Learning can be developed by learners and collaborators by way of blogs, wikis, and user-generated content. If students are doing an assignment on civics, different students could create content about a different aspect of government and share it. In the workplace, a lot of learning is informal and happens on the job. Learners could be co-authors in creating the company's overall curriculum.

Digital content technology allows us to give learners opportunities to personalize their learning and take greater control. They can pick and choose modules based on their immediate or strategic needs, they can tailor the digital content offering to the level of knowledge they require, and they can do it from anywhere they wish.

The Digital Ecosystem and Learning

The digital media ecosystem gives incredible control over how meaning and messages are developed, shared, and personalized by society. When you reflect on some of the key theories in adult learning, some obvious similarities with digital media emerge. Effective learning is personalized to the individual learner. Effective learning delivery uses different delivery methodologies based on the content. Transformative learning takes place when learners have the autonomy to process the learning in a way that makes sense to them.

While this book focuses primarily on planning and producing the multimodal aspect of digital learning content, multiplatform functionality and personalization should never be far from consideration. Chapter 2 explores these connections, considers how the brain processes media content, and suggests some universal media principles that ensure effective media content.

Digital Media and Learning: A Glove Fit

In This Chapter
- How does your brain interact with digital content?
- What are the universal content principles?
- What are some digital media mindsets?

The thought of making engaging digital learning content is intimidating for many learning professionals. Sure, anyone can pick up a microphone and record a podcast. But how do you make it interesting enough for someone to want to listen all the way to the end? And while just about anyone can shoot video on their smartphones, how do you craft a visual message that keeps learners engaged?

Making digital learning content takes work. But the learning curve for learning professionals is not as steep as many might think. Why? Because one of the most important steps is planning—defining a learning objective, breaking it down into digestible chunks, then assembling it in an order that makes sense to the learner. Then it becomes a matter of deciding whether audio, video, text, or graphics will be best to facilitate the learning. Planning digital media content is not much different from traditional instructional design, so as a learning professional you have a head start. Planning is 40 percent of the work.

What you may need to learn is how to convey a coherent message through each of these modalities, how to develop a work flow, and how to record, shoot, and edit. So if you're feeling daunted by this brave new media world, don't be. You're probably further along in your learning journey than you think.

This chapter explores the media mindset that will ensure you make engaging content and consider how your learners will make sense of your digital message. It also offers some universal media principles to guide you as you create digital learning content.

Goal of Media: Make It Quick and Easy to Understand

Most people these days want their information fast. In fact studies show that when people visit a webpage they ignore 75 percent of the words (Nielsen 2008). So, if you write a 200-word article, most folks will read only 50 of your words, if you can call that reading. And if the content doesn't immediately make sense when they read through, they'll search for another article in Google. It's not that much different with video. Visible Measures did a study in 2010 that found that 20 percent of viewers will abandon watching a video within 10 seconds of it starting; 33 percent will be gone within 30 seconds, which is not very long. People simply don't want to wait for content, and this should not surprise us. In our culture of 24-hour news and instant access to just about any information we need, we want media that's fast and easy to consume.

People working in the professional media, such as journalists, audio and video producers, and editors, are schooled in crafting content that is quick and easy to understand. In the world of nanolearning and just-in-time training, learning professionals also need to adopt this approach. So how can you review content to be sure it's quick and easy to understand? Science can help explain.

Digital Content and the Brain

It's tempting to think that making digital content is about using the latest technology, such as a video camera, new software, or a microphone. Some may think that simply pressing start on their audio recorder and talking about whatever comes to mind will lead to an engaging podcast. Or that learning the features of Adobe Photoshop, rather than visual design techniques, is all it takes to be a creative graphic designer. It's like the trainer who wants to flip the classroom and devotes her time to learning iMovie rather than the craft of bolting pictures together to construct a coherent message.

Learning how to use new technology is certainly important. It enables the real work of digital media: to help readers, viewers, and listeners make sense of your message. But learning how to communicate and shape your message is actually more important than learning all the extra features of your $1,500 camera. Effective communication requires a basic understanding of how the brain creates meaning.

Knowledge formation takes place in the learner's brain, where he builds mental models to make sense of the world. Mental models, first proposed by Swiss psychologist Jean Piaget as schema, are abstract models that represent the real world by drawing together memories into a pattern. Mental models, built from instincts, experiences, and memories, help us make sense of the world, thus playing an essential role in survival. A very basic mental model is that we need food to survive. The hunger pains we feel before lunch are interpreted through this basic mental model to tell us to go eat. Another mental model is that when we see a red traffic light, we stop. Seeing the red light may mean nothing on its own, but interpreted through this more complex mental model, we know the road rules tell us to stop when the light is red.

As a matter of survival, our brains constantly refine existing mental models and build new ones. For example, consider a friend who says nasty things behind your back. At first you won't believe it because your mental model of that person tells you she's a friend and wouldn't say such things. However, if you find more evidence, your mental model will change.

When learners listen to, read, or view your digital content, they use their experiences and memories to interpret your message. When a learner hears you talking about a bus trip on your podcast, she pieces together a picture in her mind of that trip by visualizing her own experience of being on a bus. When she sees a learning video of snow falling, she will draw on her memories of snow, how it is cold and wet, and match that with the messages she is taking in from your video. (This is why it is so important to have a good idea of the types of experiences your learner is likely to have to interpret your content. This knowledge should influence word choice and even the analogies or examples you share to bring content alive.)

Of course it gets tricky because mental models, which at first seem straightforward, are complex, especially when it comes to the construction of meaning. For example, use the phrase, "We're expecting snow," to someone from Minneapolis and they will most likely consider it a burden. Someone from the Caribbean, on the other hand, may see it as a delight.

How Your Learner's Brain Makes Sense of the World

This process in which the learner matches experience with your message can be helpfully explained by the Multi-Store Memory Model (Atkinson and Shiffrin 1968). Despite being more than half a century old, this model is still one of the best ways to understand what happens when we take information into our brains. While different aspects of this model have changed, such as terminology used to describe parts of the process and the capacity of different stages of memory, it is widely used to make sense of what happens with learning and media.

Why memories and not messages? That's because the brain thinks in memories. Everything you see, hear, feel, taste, or smell becomes a memory your brain uses to make sense of the world. Imagine you just saw a car drive by as you walk along the street. That car is now a memory. Digital media uses audio and visual memories.

Richard Atkinson and Richard Shiffrin suggest that new memories are processed in three stages, which describe a process, not a physical location in the brain. The first stage is the sensory register, also referred to by some theorists as the sensory memory. The second stage is called the working memory, also referred to as the short-term memory. The third stage is the long-term memory.

New memories, such as the visual memory of the car that just drove by, come into the brain through the sensory register, which determines whether that memory is relevant. If it is, the memory passes into the second stage: the working memory. In a sense, the sensory register acts as a gatekeeper to keep irrelevant, useless information out of the working memory to avoid overloading it. For example, you are walking along the road and see a newspaper stand but you don't want to buy a newspaper. Your sensory register discards that memory almost immediately. However, if you are walking along the road, feeling slight pangs of hunger, and you see a hotdog stand, your sensory memory may consider it important. It would then pass that into the working memory, where you think about buying a hotdog.

Sensory Register

There are a number of theories about how long it takes the sensory memory to determine what memories to allow through to the working memory. Sperling (1960) suggested that for visual memories it could be a fraction of a second, while Baddely (1999) suggested that for auditory memories it could be two to three seconds. Without being specific about the exact amount of time, which may evolve with subsequent studies, what is clear now is that the time it takes to decide what to pass into the working and long-term memory is very short.

The practical implication for creating digital content is huge. Voice-over scripts with redundant words are useless clutter that increase the work of the sensory memory, slowing down the speed of comprehension. Elements in a graphic or video frame that do not contribute to the message increase the work the brain must complete to understand the message (Figure 2-1). The digital communicator must be disciplined to reduce sensory clutter.

Figure 2-1. A Cluttered and an Uncluttered Frame

The image on the left is filled with distracting objects. The image on the right has much less clutter, so the brain can process it more quickly.

The Working Memory

The working memory can be described as the space where you think about what's happening around you. The car that drives by finds its way into the working memory because you recognize a friend driving it. The working memory draws on long-term memories (mental models) as well as what's in front of you to make sense of what is going on.

As with the sensory register, theorists differ in how they believe the working memory functions and its capacity. Some measure its capacity in duration, while others quantify it in terms of how many chunks of information it can hold. Many educators are familiar with the magic seven formula originally proposed by George A. Miller in the 1950s, which suggests we can remember seven chunks of information, plus or minus two. This was taught in train-the-trainer classes and teacher education programs well into the 1990s. However, more recent studies suggest the brain has a smaller capacity: Cowan (2001) finds it to be closer to between three and five meaningful items.

This leads to cognitive load theory and how much the brain can process without being over-loaded (Sweller 1988). When cognitive load is too high, learners might experience difficulty in processing and understanding information. What's important for digital communicators to remember is that the human brain has a limited capacity to process lots of information at one time.

Sensory Memory Is Linked to Survival

During a recent media workshop in New York City, I asked participants to form pairs and head out into Times Square with me. One person in each pair closed his eyes and described everything he could remember from around him in this iconic location. The second person wrote it down. People remembered things like a neon sign, a café table, the discount theater ticket booth, and sometimes the smell of a hotdog stand. On average, participants remembered between 10 and 15 things. Then we looked around to see that they had missed thousands of sights, sounds, and even smells. This is a powerful example of how efficient the sensory register is at discarding irrelevant information.

Long-Term Memory

The long-term memory is where we store all our memories as mental models. From a biological perspective, memory is formed by regularly firing neurons that form associations and networks with other neurons—this is known as long-term potentiation.

Most educators don't need brain science to tell them that role plays, rehearsals, experiments, and other active tasks make it easier for learners to remember content. You've been doing this for years, right? Outside the learning world, this act of processing through rehearsal has been a critical skill. Actors rehearse their lines. Kids study flash cards to remember their times tables for math class. Neuroscience simply helps us understand the importance of moving in and out of the stages of memory. Anything that has a degree of rehearsal will reinforce that memory. To be sure, there's still much to learn about memory development, but there are two clear implications for digital educators.

First, the more the learner can rehearse what she has learned, the more likely she will remember it. That's why flash cards and times tables are used in school. However, digital media content creators are at a distinct disadvantage because we have no control over whether learners rehearse what they learn.

So in its place we need to build repetition into our content. Consider how marketing professionals do this. Infomercials repeat a toll-free phone number four or five times, while car manufacturers and soda makers run their ads many, many times in hopes that after a few viewings the message will stick.

Second, your learners use their experiences (mental models) to understand your message. These experiences include culture, life story, language, education, and even different interpretations of the same word. So it's imperative to get a feeling for how your audience may interpret your message before you finalize any content.

Survival Instincts

The three-stage memory model is helpful for understanding how your learners will process what you teach them, whether that be in a classroom or through digital content. But it also presents a dilemma. If the sensory register is designed to discard most of the sensory stimulus it encounters, how can you ensure your content gets through to the working memory and is not discarded with everything else?

The human brain is wired for survival, as are most animals. So people are on constant alert for anything that may be a threat. Humans like to have an element of control over their environment and for their lives to be calm, certain, and predictable. Anytime that is threatened, they are triggered into an alert status. For example, consider a woman sitting one afternoon at an outdoor café, reading a novel and sipping on a latte. When a nearby car screeches around the corner, her head snaps up and she becomes very alert. Her heart starts pumping faster, preparing the muscles in her body to jump out of the way or react in some other manner. She looks to see what is happening and wants to know if it is a threat. Of course, physical dangers are not the only thing that put us on the defense. Anything that changes or disrupts a human's sense of control will increase alertness. Consider when a CEO announces a restructure. This change is a major threat not only to the certainty and predictability of how people work in the organization, but also to their income and survival.

So does this mean you have to pepper your digital content with threats? Not quite. Over the years, practitioners in traditional media have instinctively known that any time you change something, it will get most people's attention. This is why good voice-over artists constantly change their pitch, pace, and volume. They pause to disrupt the flow of a phrase and create an emphasis. At the pause, the listener stops and refocuses attention so the orator can make a point. It's why morning radio shows have more than one presenter—if one person is speaking and the other chimes in, it creates variety and grabs attention. In addition to keeping attention, anytime there is a perceived change it creates the sense that you are missing something, which again draws your attention.

So change is an important currency in digital media content because it's what you use to keep learners' attention and trick them into thinking that if they discard the information, they'll be missing something. You'll see that the importance of change is incorporated into many of the techniques shared throughout this book.

Universal Content Principles

So what do all of these ideas mean when it comes to making engaging digital learning content that is quick to understand and easy to remember? Here are six universal principles of good media that will help you shape content for your learners' brains. These apply to all aspects of your content whether it be the words you choose, background music, or overall package:

- **The Short Principle: Keep content as short as possible without compromising the integrity of the message.** This applies to all elements of your message, such as individual words, sounds, graphics, or shots, as well as the overall package. The shorter each element is, the quicker the sensory memory will process it. And media and learning consumers are generally impatient when seeking information, so overall content should be kept short. There is no specific length for the perfect video, podcast, or piece of written text. Instead it should be determined by the content, the audience, and the question, "Is this as short as it possibly can be?"
- **The Simple Principle: Make sure content is not difficult to understand.** If your learner has to scratch his head trying to figure out something while the video or podcast continues, the content needs to be simplified. Don't complicate your message with multiple purposes. Stick to one learning objective and use it as a yardstick to remove anything not relevant. Some approach media asking, "How much can I put in?" It's more helpful to ask, "How much can I take out without compromising my objectives?"
- **The Familiarity Principle: Draw on the audience's memories and experiences.** It's easy to think, "This makes sense to me." This is why video content on organizational change often fails. If messages are produced by people with MBAs who use jargon like vertical integration and the like, factory floor workers will not understand because they use different mental models to make sense of such terms. In some cases they may not have the memories to understand the jargon. Of course it works the other way as well: Content needs to use words, expressions, stories, and media elements that are familiar to the learner.
- **The Emotion Principle: Increase engagement by tapping into emotions such as humor, happiness, and tension.** Consider how to use elements like music, sound effects, words and phrases, and images. Use techniques such as camera angle, shot size, editing style, and the rule of thirds.
- **The Creative Repetition Principle: Repeat key points but do them differently each time.** Repetition leads to memory retention. However, if you repeat the same thing over and over again, there is no change, and the audience will zone out. So repeat the key point but vary it every time.

- **The Change Principle: Keep changing the way you communicate.** Anything that stays the same will cause the learner to zone out. To avoid that, incorporate change—for example, keep changing shots in videos, music in podcasts, and vocal pace and pitch in voice-overs as appropriate.

Digital Media Mindsets

Creating good content is not just about adhering blindly to a few principles. It's also about adopting a digital communicator's mindset. Here are three mindsets that lead to more engaging content.

- **Modality Sensitivity: Look for the best modality to most powerfully convey your message.** This has two aspects. First, multimodal communicators choose the modality that best works for the topic, not the one they personally like or are familiar with. The digital ecosystem liberates you from using only video as in TV, only text as in newspapers and magazines, or only audio as in radio for learning. If you need to show someone how to do something, like use a piece of equipment, you should use video. Second, when a modality is chosen, digital communicators exploit all it has to offer. If you're creating learning podcasts, it's easy just to switch on the microphone and speak. But audio offers two additional storytelling tools: music and sound effects. They can make the content more lively and engaging. The digital communicator not only chooses the best modality for the topic, but also uses everything it offers to make the message stand out.

- **Platform Sensitivity: Craft content so it works well for the platform it is being consumed on.** Not every piece of digital learning content will be viewed on a desktop computer. Some learners will read your job aid on a smartphone. Smartphones are really useful because they take your content anywhere there's a cell signal. However, they are clumsier to use than a desktop. Hyperlinks and buttons are pressed by fingers that don't have the precision of a mouse. Content might be viewed outside under a strong sun. The screens are much smaller, which means text is harder to read and graphics are harder to decipher. A PDF that looks good when printed will be very difficult to read on a smartphone screen. So identify the most common device people will use to access content and design the content so it is easy to consume on that platform. If it's a smartphone, use bigger fonts and make the graphics larger. Create bigger buttons for fingers. Use less text. If learners will be accessing your content across multiple platforms, it is ideal to produce a different version for each platform. Yes, that can be expensive, but that's true platform sensitivity. If you don't have the budget to do so, go for the lowest common denominator or use responsive design techniques.

- **Personalization: Give learners choices to manage their learning.** One of the biggest changes to media consumption since the digital revolution has been the shift of control from the publisher to the consumer. For example, a TV program director once decided what time you would watch a hit TV show. Now you can watch your favorite shows on demand by going to the channel's website. When you log in to your favorite news site while traveling, it won't offer the weather forecast back home but for your current location. Personalization means always asking what you can do to be more focused and targeted, rather than broad. This could mean creating different versions of the same content for different users. It might mean designing your learning management system architecture to let people skip over content that simply regurgitates prior learning. It also means building in as much interactivity as you can.

Summary

As you progress through this book, you'll see that the universal principles and digital media mindset underpin the techniques found within its pages. While there is much to learn to truly master the art of crafting digital content that goes beyond just a point-and-shoot video or a rambling podcast, learning professionals are uniquely suited to craft this content. Learning, like media, is about taking complex information and making it easy for the learner to make sense of. But crafting engaging content is only part of the story. Digital communicators also need to know how to efficiently work through each step of the production process, which we'll tackle in the next chapter.

Creating Digital Media Fast and Affordably

In This Chapter

- How can a consistent work flow speed up production and improve content quality?
- What are the elements of a good digital work flow?
- How can the rapid media technique work flow help you create fabulous digital learning content fast and affordably?

This book aims to help you make digital learning content that's engaging, quick to produce, and affordable. Chapter 2 examined what makes engaging digital content by exploring how the brain works and considering universal principles of good content. Good digital content should captivate the learner, be understandable, and easy to remember. But we haven't covered the fast or affordable aspects yet.

As a learning professional, your primary job is not making digital media content. It is helping people learn. Making digital learning content is just one of many methods you'll use every week to develop people. It's part of your professional toolkit along with skills such as coaching, leading classroom discussions, and facilitating learning activities. In the demands of today's workplace, most will not have the luxury of approaching the business of making digital learning content the way an artist has when she leisurely wonders down to the seaside to paint a sunset.

Learning professionals spend many hours on the road, attend endless corporate meetings, and play tug-of-war with administrative duties like timesheets, assessments, and expense reports. This juggling act means that if they want to make digital learning content, they have to do it fast without compromising quality.

And while learning professionals must make it fast, they generally have to do it on a shoestring budget. They don't work in Hollywood, where the budget for a single camera is in the tens of thousands of dollars (and up). Many shoot digital video on cameras from Amazon that cost less than $300 and, if they're lucky, come with a free external microphone. Others produce podcasts using apps on their smartphones. And just as expensive cameras aren't an option for learning departments, few have the budget for fancy editing programs or time to attend the training classes that will teach them to edit like a media professional. So they have to make content affordably, but without compromising the quality.

The way to achieve all this—make quality content fast and without breaking the bank—is to develop an effective work flow for the steps to get a task done and the consistent order you follow when doing so. Effective work flow is important for most tasks. For example, if you're applying for a mortgage, the first step is to fill out some paperwork. Then a loan officer will conduct a credit check. If your credit score is sufficient, they will calculate your debt to income ratio to determine how much you can afford. Then they will require paperwork, such as your tax return or a pay stub to prove your income. Everything is done in an orderly and carefully managed way. If the loan officer gets sick or takes a promotion, a new loan officer can quickly jump in and take over the process because this explicit set of steps is followed by everyone handling mortgage applications.

When you get to more creative tasks like creating digital content, the steps may seem less clear, although you still follow a process. You start with a purpose for your message and consider how you will achieve that: Will it be by interviewing someone, researching some background material, or another approach? You break down your message into a series of chunks and put it into a sequence that will make sense to your learner. Then you record, shoot, draw, or write the content. After this, you review it, check its accuracy, and sign off on it.

After you follow a work flow a few times, it becomes a habit. The more you follow it, the more entrenched the steps become, and you will find it becomes automatic—just like making your morning coffee. When you stumble into the kitchen each morning, wondering why the alarm clock went off earlier than it should have, do you grind the coffee beans first or boil the water? Whatever your approach, you probably do it the same way every morning.

Work Flow Leads to Excellence

In my experience, people and organizations without an effective work flow take longer to make content and struggle to consistently produce truly engaging content. I've seen this in newspaper companies transitioning to the digital ecosystem as well as nonmedia companies adopting video or audio into their learning departments. The more explicit their work flow, the better teams work together. The more effective the sequence of that work flow, the faster they make their content.

When it comes to a complex task like creating media content, following an inefficient work flow that has a poor sequence can add unnecessary time. When you're making your morning coffee, it may be quicker to boil the water first before grinding the coffee beans because you can grind the beans while the water is heating up, saving you a few extra moments to read the newspaper or get dressed.

But sometimes it's not always obvious which steps to do first to improve production time. For example, you'll notice that when we discuss video work flow later in the book, drawing the storyboard comes before writing the script. While this seems counterintuitive, it actually shaves considerable time off the production process and helps ensure each shot flows from one to another without looking inconsistent. Getting the order right in a work flow can make a huge difference in terms of efficiency. If you're busy designing classes, attending meetings, and all those other things that learning professionals juggle every week, wouldn't it be nice to save three hours? An effective production work flow will help with that.

Some people don't have a work flow at all because they produce podcasts or videos so rarely they just think it up as they go along. But this path to digital content is rife with stumbling blocks. They may grab their camera and head out to a shoot only to realize once they get there that the light is inadequate. So they either have to wait until the following day when there's more natural light or head back to their office to grab a lighting kit. It's a little like cooking—if you're frying an egg, you get the spatula out before you crack the egg in the pan rather than hunting for it at the time it needs to be flipped, risking the yoke being overcooked.

In short, an effective work flow establishes the tasks you need to complete a project. It determines the best sequence in which to complete the project efficiently. It helps the work become a habit, thus freeing your mind to be creative. And it makes collaboration easier because all people on the team share the same expectations about when the task should be done, in which order, and to what standard.

The Rapid Media Technique

If over a few years you were to work for several different media companies, say in a series of TV newsrooms, you'd find that while each one has its own ways of doing things, most will largely follow a similar approach. The general steps will be the same across the board, but each newsroom will localize a work flow to suit that organization's culture, its technical setup, and the personalities of its editors and on-air talent.

The work flow presented in this book is based on my experience helping both media and nonmedia practitioners and organizations in more than 25 countries around the world. It comes from observing what does and does not work and helping clients develop strategies that have led to significant improvements in production and content quality. This work flow does not seek to critique other work flows or comment on localized approaches; rather, it seeks to share one that has been successful in helping many other people and organizations, especially in the learning world.

This work flow is presented so you can adopt its general steps and adapt them your own organizational context. Its emphasis is on churning out lots of content and doing it consistently to a high standard. And it is designed to help you make that content faster without compromising quality. As you know, everyone wants everything faster today, and it's no exception when business units come to the training department for support.

Buying Inexpensive Equipment

I run a two-day workshop on how to create engaging learning video using entry-level consumer cameras. Participants create videos during the class using a $260 Canon camcorder. Inevitably, one or two participants will arrive packing their expensive DSLR or $2,000 prosumer camera and then proceed to disparage the consumer cameras we use for the class. Of course they're welcome to use their cameras for the exercises, and they do. But here's what's interesting. When we review their videos at the end of the class, they are often blurry, poorly exposed, and shaky, with improper white balance. In contrast, the videos shot by participants on the cheap cameras turn out sharp, well lit, and stable. Creating quality digital content is not about how expensive your camera is. It's about how you use the equipment. It's easy to be blinded by digital toys with lots of features, but skills, work flow, and the discipline to follow it are what lead to consistently good-quality content.

The rapid media technique follows three significant stages:
1. plan
2. create
3. edit.

This work flow loosely parallels the traditional production method for film and broadcast of pre-production, production, and post-production, except it seeks to be more generalized to also include digital text and graphics. The techniques are adapted for use on affordable equipment, such as microphones or cameras you can buy on Amazon or at electronics stores. You needn't spend your entire budget on this equipment. In fact, fancy equipment can get learning professionals new to the technology into trouble because it's easy to be distracted by advanced functions that often aren't necessary for their purposes. As we explore each modality, we will look at the process of making engaging content fast and affordably through these steps. Each step will in principle be similar but, by virtue of the differences of making digital text to making video, will have different steps specific to that modality. Let's consider an overview of each stage first. We'll go into specifics for each modality later in the book.

Step 1: Plan

Planning media content is the most important stage of production, yet it is probably the most overlooked. Regardless of whether you're writing screen text or shooting video, the more time and energy you put into the planning, the better your product will be and the quicker it will be to produce. There's not a specific rule that says how much time you should spend planning content, but it's reasonable to suggest that of your overall production time, the percentage of time allocated to planning should be around 40 percent for screen text and video, 30 percent for audio, and 20 percent for graphics. The breakdown may vary depending on the topic, but if you're not putting enough time aside for planning, your content will not be as focused and you will end up spending more time to produce it.

Why is planning so important? It enables you to focus on your message and learning objective, which then becomes a yardstick to measure every element of your content to ensure that it achieves your objective. It enables you to create a production schedule that is efficient and avoid problems that can set you back, such as being told by security you can't film at a location you needed because you didn't get permission. It also gives everyone on the team, from the person holding the microphone to the person drawing the graphics, a precise set of editorial and production expectations. The more you plan your content, the more you are free during the creation stage to be creative.

To Wing It or Plan It, That Is the Question

It's tempting to wing it when it comes to producing digital content. It seems easy to skip planning the questions for a podcast interview or forget to map out what shots will convey the message in a video. The feeling is that winging it works and planning is just, well, too cumbersome and time-consuming. This is not that different to educators who decide to wing it and don't prepare lesson plans. They get away with it in the classroom because they're naturally gifted in classroom management or their topic. So the adrenalin kicks in and gives them what they need to deliver a decent result. But adrenalin dries up after a while and winging it is not sustainable over the long term. The same goes for media production. It won't be long before your ability to consistently churn out engaging content dries up. The only way to regularly turn out good content is to plan it, which allows you to redeploy your natural improvisational skills into being creative within your plan as you record audio, shoot video, or take photographs.

Each modality demands different approaches to planning. However, planning generally involves editorial tasks such as developing the learning objective, breaking content into digestible chunks, and creating narrative structures appropriate for your audience. You'll complete logistics such as conducting research; booking interviews; getting permissions or clearing copyright for graphics, music, and artists; and drawing up shot plans.

Step 2: Create

Creating content is what most people traditionally associate with media production. It's filming, recording audio, writing the blog post, and drawing the graphics. The focus for this stage of production is doing everything right and allowing your creativity to sweeten it. If you're producing a podcast interview, you must record the audio clearly and at the right level with the microphone positioned correctly. If you're taking a photo to drop into a presentation, you must ensure that your subject or object is well lit and clearly in focus. When shooting video, correct focus, lighting, and audio are crucial.

The reason it is important to do everything right during the create stage is because correcting mistakes when you move on to editing wastes time. In fact, if you're really unlucky, you may have to go back and reshoot your pictures or rerecord your interview. Even correcting simple mistakes such as an underexposed shot wastes time in the edit stage that could be spent being creative. The best way to ensure that you create content right the first time is to plan your content and then minimize the times you have to improvise to capture the content.

Working With Subject Matter Experts

If you're working with subject matter experts (SMEs), make sure they sign off on each step of the project. And agree with them at the outset that once they have signed off, there are no revisions. If you leave it open-ended without having them sign off at specific points, your project could go on forever if they change their mind. I've had experiences in which SMEs turn to the learning producer and say, "I don't like this; we need to start again." It's an impossible situation to be in, but had my clients set up sign-off stages they could have turned to the SME and said, "Sorry, you'll have to take a ticket and wait in line." Learning producers should be accountable for creating great content, but the accuracy of the content should come down to the SME.

Creating digital content requires skills too, which take time to learn. If you have planned everything well, your mind will be free to be creative. Instead of just reading your list of questions for a podcast interview, you'll have the mental bandwidth to listen to patterns of answers and generate new lines of inquiry to draw out the talent. In addition to shooting what's required on the storyboard, you'll have the brain space to recognize other visual opportunities on location that you may not have been able to anticipate while planning, which might give the shot more pizzazz.

Ultimately, if you plan your content well and create it correctly, you set yourself up to save a lot of time in the edit stage.

Step 3: Edit

Editing digital content is the final stage of the rapid media technique. Similar to creating your content, the process for editing each modality is unique. Editing audio is about cutting out unnecessary words or phrases and adding music and sound effects where appropriate. Editing video is about positioning shots along a timeline, trimming them so they flow together, and adding things like music and effects. Editing graphics involves preparing the final image for inclusion in an article or video. And editing digital text involves looking at structure, accuracy, grammar, and spelling, as well as integrating other modalities into the narrative.

The key to good editing is being organized and disciplined. In fact, the better your administrative systems are and the more disciplined you are at sticking to them, the faster you will be able to edit. The vision of an uber-organized practitioner may clash with the romanticized notion of the creative editor who doesn't wear socks and works late into the night. But talk to the best editors and you'll find the reason they can be creative is because they have procedures for organizing digital assets, file name conventions to manage different versions of their product, and other systems that stop them from losing content, getting confused, or feeling bogged down. Their excellent organization frees their minds to let their talent shine.

Good editors are good with software. Understanding software like MS Word, Adobe Acrobat, Scrivener, and InDesign is important, as is using content and learning management systems. For audio producers, knowing file types and audio editing software is crucial. Video editors need to be skillful at video editing programs and advanced tools like After Effects, while graphic designers need to know their way around Photoshop.

Summary

Work flows can have their limitations, and it's fair to acknowledge them. Often circumstances will change and you need to be flexible in your approach. For example, you may be called to create content with little notice or in response to a last-minute opportunity. This doesn't allow you to do extensive planning, so you are required to improvise. You're not going to turn down an opportunity simply because you didn't get a chance to do a shot plan or set up a series of interview questions. At times, going with the flow is necessary. There's an old saying, "Rules are for the blind obedience of fools and the guidance of the wise." There's a lot of truth in this—along with some danger. Be flexible but don't allow this flexibility to be an excuse to avoid a work flow. Not following a work flow will inevitably require more correctional work at the end of the process.

Having discussed the dynamics of digital media, the way the brain deals with media content, and the work flow for making engaging content affordably, it's time to get specific. The following chapters will explore each step of the rapid media work flow for each of the four modalities: audio, video, graphics, and screen text. We'll explore how each modality works in a learning context, look at what to plan before you start creating, decide on what equipment you need for production, and walk through the practical steps of creating it and how to edit it.

Audio and Learning

In This Chapter

- When should you use audio in learning materials?
- What are the three communication tools of audio?
- How do the universal content principles apply to audio?
- What does an audio work flow look like?

When you hear people discussing media content in learning, such as blended learning or the flipped classroom, a good chunk of those conversations zero in on how to leverage video without referencing what other modalities like audio offer. This is a shame. Despite all video has to offer, which we'll cover in the next section of the book, it often overshadows the amazing opportunities audio also offers to learning professionals.

Audio as a modality for learning has been around a long time. Traditionally, listeners received it through their radio or on clunky old devices like cassette players and cartridge machines. Today learners can listen to audio from podcasts, streaming audio, and even audio embedded in other media such as slideshows. These new platforms offer incredible opportunities to easily make learning available on demand. No longer do learners have to wait for a 10 p.m. radio lecture or go rummaging around their bag to find the cassette tape of a lecture they missed—they simply open a file on their smartphone or tablet or look up a webpage and they've got it.

Audio and learning first paired up in the 1920s. In the United States, the short-lived pioneer radio station WGI, in Massachusetts, broadcast lectures from professors at Tufts College in 1922, while the British Broadcasting Company—later the BBC—did its first broadcast to school-children in 1924 (Das 2007). It quickly became a fixture for broadcasters around the world as radio pioneers developed ways to make radio an intrinsic part of everyday life. Using radio for education became formalized in 1929, when Ohio State University started the *School of the Air*, while on the other side of the world, the Australian Broadcasting Commission launched Schools Broadcasts to support classroom instruction in traditional schools. Both are early examples of what we might today call blended learning programs using technology. In 1930, CBS launched its weekly half-hour show, *American School of the Air*, followed soon after by NBC's *University of the Air* (Das 2007).

Audio has played a key role in educating people around the world, particularly in countries with large landmasses and sparse populations like Australia, as well as in developing countries, where radio offered the opportunity to reach millions. In the late 1940s, Australia launched the *School of the Air* for children living on remote ranches in the dusty outback who were too far from schools to attend in person. And from the 1950s, UNESCO rolled out educational radio to developing countries such as India, Pakistan, and Thailand (Das 2007; UNESCO n.d.; Big Black Dog Communications 2016).

Despite audio being overshadowed by its more glamorous cousin, video, its consumption has quietly grown and will most likely continue, especially as more and more devices become connected to the Internet. Whether it's consumed as a radio broadcast, a podcast, or streamed over the Internet, audio is quick and easy to produce and costs very little to put together. It's portable and can be enjoyed while people do other tasks such as driving, working out, or sitting at an airport waiting for a flight.

Audio is a powerful tool to help people learn, especially because it can be distributed in so many forms. This book will refer to audio mostly as a podcast because that's what most learning professionals will be producing. However, the work flow, equipment, and skills necessary to create compelling learning podcasts are the same as the ones you will need when creating other forms of audio.

Distributing Digital Audio to Your Learners

Digital audio content can be shared across many platforms—desktop computers, smartphones, and even in the classroom if you have a device that can connect to speakers. As a digital educator you'll need to consider how to distribute it to your learners. The most common options open to you are the following:

- email
- web link
- podcast
- online streaming, either live or on demand
- embedded in another product
- learning management system (LMS).

Email

It's easy to take your audio file and email it to your learners. It's a simple approach, especially if you already have an email list. However, it is not always convenient for learners because some may have limitations placed by their IT department on the type of email attachments they can accept. Also, as email programs become more sophisticated in blocking spam, some emails may end up in the spam or clutter folders.

Web Link

You could save your audio file in the cloud, such as in a folder on Dropbox, Hightail, or OneDrive. Then either invite learners to access the folder with the audio file or send them a link they can use to play the file in a browser or download it. This is quick, easy, and convenient for one-offs. But it's not conducive to longer programs of learning that require you to monitor who is downloading and using the content.

Podcast

A podcast is a series of audio programs that are automatically downloaded over the Internet through subscription services like RSS. Podcast episodes are stored on hosting sites such as Spreaker, SoundCloud, Ourmedia, and PodOmatic and marketed through podcast directories such as iTunes, doubleTwist, and Stitcher. Some podcast hosts are free while others charge a fee, and you'll need to create an account with the host. When you upload files to directories, they will ask for the title, the RSS feed, cover artwork, and other things such as your email and web address and Twitter handle. Podcasts were born as audio content but when video came to the web, people started to use the term for video as well, and even for PDF episodes that were automatically downloaded. This book follows the original definition.

Online Streaming

Streaming refers to audio content playing live over the Internet rather than a single downloaded file. Streaming can be delivered on demand or continuously, such as the live feed from a radio station. To stream audio you need to have accounts with streaming providers, and the costs can range from hundreds to thousands of dollars depending on which company you use. Many of these providers will give you the option to customize your audio player, which you would embed on your website or intranet, or within the content management system. Many providers also offer monetizing opportunities so you can charge a fee for learners to access your media, which is good for edu-preneurs such as professional speakers, authors, and seminar leaders. Streaming is good if you want to deliver a live masterclass or massive open online course (MOOC), or when you want learners to choose their modules at will.

Embedded in Another Product

You can also distribute audio within other media products, such as PowerPoint. At a simplified level, you embed pre-recorded audio into the slide deck, then click on "Create Video." The pre-recorded audio could be of you speaking to slides. The "Create Video" function will automatically advance the slides with your audio. Strictly speaking, this is not really a video, despite it being saved as a video file, because it doesn't show moving action.

Software programs such as Articulate or TechSmith's Camtasia have built-in audio editing facilities to manipulate audio that accompanies screen captures, slide decks, and other content. You also have the option to create audio with commentary and music outside these programs in a dedicated audio editing program, such as Audacity or Sound Forge, and import the audio file to match the slides.

Learning Management System

You might load the audio into your LMS for learners to access. Different systems will handle audio differently, but you'll upload it as part of the process for making learning content. An LMS allows you to monitor what's being consumed, an ideal situation for publishing and distributing audio.

When to Use Audio for Learning

Radio has often been described as the "theater of the mind," because the message plays out visually in the listener's mind. This phrase equally applies to audio experienced as a podcast or streamed over the Internet. To make sense of your audio message, the listener draws on his memory and imagination to craft a picture on a virtual screen inside his head. The magic of audio is that your listener takes significantly more ownership of this picture because he builds on it with his experiences, ideas, and mindset.

Let's say you produce a podcast on workplace conflict that deals with the effects of value judgments in professional relationships. As you describe a judgmental comment that inflamed a workplace relationship, your listener will draw on her own experiences of either being in a similar conflict or having seen one to paint a picture in her mind of what you are talking about. It's no longer your description but hers, no longer a hypothetical situation but something that feels much more real to her. Audio works very well for topics that require learners to draw on memories, experiences, and ideas they already have. However, it struggles with topics for which they can't draw on pre-existing memories. Topics that don't work well in audio tend to include a high degree of detail and complexity.

Let's say you're teaching video camera operators about the Kelvin scale so they can set the white balance on their camera. It's unlikely they'll remember hard facts such as what range cool colors are on the Kelvin scale and what range warm colors are. An everyday example of this is how listeners remember stories on the radio but forget details. How often have you listened to a weather update but then almost immediately forgotten the actual temperature? It's easy to forget the specifics, but when the announcer says, "Don't forget to pack your umbrella," you tend to remember.

Listeners Visualize What They Hear

Many years ago, a former radio colleague told me her listeners got a shock when they met her in person. "They looked stunned so I started to ask them why." She went on to say, "Turns out most thought I was tall and blonde." She was short with auburn hair. This is a good example of how listeners instinctively create visual pictures of who they hear and what the person is talking about. Usually their visual image of the person will reflect what they hope or expect the person to look like. It's not just people they visualize. Talk about going to a café and they'll imagine themselves sipping a chai latte in their favorite local café. They'll even smell the chai spices. Talk about the beach and an image of their favorite resort will pop into their heads. This is the magic of audio. Every message is personalized with the listener's experiences and emotions. Audio engages the listener with the message. Video simply presents it.

Communication Tools of Audio

There's a sense in which creating audio messages is like painting pictures in the listeners' minds. And just as an artist has a set of tools to paint a picture, audio communicators have tools too. But instead of brushes, colors, and canvas, the audio communicator uses:

- words
- music
- sound effects.

It's easy to use only spoken word in your audio. However, your content will be more engaging if you go beyond the spoken word by engaging your learners' emotions with music and drawing on their long-term memory with sound effects.

The Spoken Word

The spoken word is the heartbeat of audio communication and is good for conveying concrete details that are less open to interpretation. An artist will use a fine paintbrush to add specific detail to an important part of the picture's message, such as a facial expression. Likewise, the podcaster will use spoken word to convey more concrete information that cannot be easily conveyed by music or sound effects.

For example, the sound effect of a waterfall may help you visualize one, but it won't convey where it is and why it's important. The spoken word can answer these questions more directly.

While the spoken word is good for detail, it can be slow to get some information across. For example, funereal music may tell your listener things are grim quicker, and more elegantly, than saying, "It was a gloomy day and no one was feeling happy."

Music

Music for the audio communicator is like the palette of paint an artist uses to splash color and life onto the canvas. Music influences mood. If you want listeners to feel sad, relaxed, happy, or excited, there is a piece of music that will do that for you. Music influences energy levels. Just when a podcast starts to drag, a short infusion of up-tempo music can lift the pace. And music creates atmosphere, transporting you anywhere in the world. Playing "Take Me Out to the Ball Game" with the sound effect of a crowd roaring can instantly transport your listeners to the ballpark.

When it comes to digital learning content, music does not exist for entertainment. Instead it plays a supporting role to affect mood, energy, and atmosphere. For example, if you want people to feel inspired about what they will learn in a podcast, you could start a podcast with a positive, uplifting piece of music. If you have produced a podcast about cultural customs to respect when traveling to Tokyo, you might use music written in a pentatonic scale, which is common in Japan, to set the scene for the country you are focusing on. If your podcast is longer than a few minutes, you could insert short music tracks at various intervals to give the listener a break to consolidate what they hear.

Sound Effects

To paint a backdrop such as the sky or a sunset, the artist might pick up a broad brush and get to work. An audio professional uses sound effects in the same way. Sound effects create atmosphere and attract the listener's attention. They trigger long-term memories, adding life to your message. Their speed at communicating can be helpful too. If you hear the sound of traffic noise and honking horns, most people will immediately think of New York or another busy city. It's quicker and less clumsy than planning a voice-over with, "And now we go to New York . . ."

Sound effects are broad rather than specific, so often they will only convey part of the message. They may transport the listener somewhere but they won't tell the listener why or what they're doing. The sound effects generally need to be combined with words and music for an immersive effect.

Universal Content Principles for Audio

In chapter 2, we listed some universal principles of good content that can apply to audio, video, and screen text. What do they look like when it comes to audio content?

- **The Short Principle: Audio content should be short and snappy.** A lot of commercial radio stations limit interviews to between two and three minutes because people lose concentration fast. If you have lots of talking in your podcast, break it up with music. Or break the overall podcast into several shorter modules.
- **The Simple Principle: Do not overload the listener with content.** Use simple words that are quick and easy for your listeners to recognize and process. And stick to one learning objective.

- **The Familiarity Principle: Media elements need to be familiar to your listeners, so use words, stories, and analogies they recognize.** Choose sound effects that they can relate to. And make sure your music is what your listeners expect. Glenn Miller music in the background may not be effective for Generation Y listeners unless you want to create a flashback.
- **The Emotion Principle: Use music to influence your listeners' energy levels.** Use words, phrases, and stories you know will appeal to them.
- **The Creative Repetition Principle: Repeat key learning points, but each time you repeat them, do so differently.** For example, use a voice-over, then a sound bite from a subject matter expert, and then perhaps a role play.
- **The Change Principle: Variety keeps people listening.** Consider how you can add aural variety to your podcast. For instance, you could use two presenters. Or you could change the music throughout the podcast and add sound effects. Also consider changing between content techniques—you could feature an interview, a role play, and a monologue rather than just a monologue. Of course, it's important not to overdo the change and have new music every 15 seconds. So what makes the ideal number of changes? This is where the art comes into play; rather than settle on something concrete, like "change every 20 seconds," it's probably more useful to review your content and minimize the change when it distracts from the learning.

How Long Should Digital Learning Audio Content Be?

Is there a perfect duration for a podcast or element of audio learning? Not really. The answer depends entirely on the content and how it is produced. It's easy to suggest you talk no longer than three minutes at a time, which is appropriate for most situations. However, some presenters are magically engaging and could keep you enthralled for 20 minutes. So how do we gauge the perfect length? My advice is to ask a question: "Can I make this shorter?" Be ruthless with your answer and keep cutting until taking something out would ruin your message.

The Digital Mindset and Audio

When it comes to the digital mindset, there are three questions to ask:
- What's the best modality to convey the content?
- What platform will the learner access this content on?
- How can the learner personalize the content?

The audio modality is effective when your listeners have knowledge and experience to tap into with the spoken word, music, and sound effects. This is when you might choose a podcast, not because it's fun to create or quick and easy to turn around. When a learning topic requires you to convey a lot of detailed information, such as facts and figures, you should avoid podcasts and instead opt for a more appropriate modality such as digital text. Podcasts are great for soft skills training such as sales or leadership, but not as good for more specific topics such as IT, science, or finance.

The platform your learner will access the podcast on should also influence how you produce the content. The considerations are subtler for podcasts than they are for video, although still important. For example, if you know learners will mostly listen when driving in a car, you might use softer sound effects because cars tend to be soundproofed and learners will have fewer auditory distractions. However, if they're likely to be listening in a factory or at an airport waiting for a flight, you might rely less on quieter sound effects that are easily drowned out by noisy environments.

Transformative learning is personal and the digital communicator considers how the podcast can be used in a way that mostly fits the learner's pace and schedule. What can you do to allow the learner to fit the podcast around his life? Perhaps you can offer two versions of the podcast: one that's complete and a second that is broken into modules. With modules the learner can pace the podcast differently, or skip ones that cover material he is already familiar with. You can also use technology to allow him to set the time that podcast modules are pushed out to him.

An Audio Work Flow

We've discussed why audio is good for learning, how to play to its strengths, and the three communication tools you have to help people learn. But how do you actually build audio content? It's important to follow a consistent work flow that ensures the right steps are taken in the right order. There is no perfect work flow, although there are many that are far from effective. This book explores production through the lens of the plan, create, and edit work flow. Here's how it looks for podcasts.

Step One: Planning

1. Set the learning objective.
2. Break the objective into knowledge chunks.
3. Create a structure for the content.
4. Determine which format to use. For instance, will you record a monologue, interview a subject matter expert, or facilitate a panel?
5. Write scripts, plan interviews, and choose music and sound effects.
6. Conduct basic administration tasks, such as copyright checks.

Step Two: Creating

1. Record interviews using your computer, digital audio recorder, or smart device.

Step Three: Editing
1. Edit spoken word content.
2. Process audio.
3. Add music and sound effects using multitrack.
4. Publish.

Summary

Audio offers powerful learning opportunities because the learner crafts the message using her memory and imagination, making it far more personal. It is especially effective for content that requires the learner to reflect on her experiences. However, it struggles to teach content with lots of facts and figures. The learning professional who creates podcasts or streamed audio content for learning will weave together the spoken word, music, and sound effects to convey the message. His aim will be to keep the content short and simple and engage creative repetition to increase retention.

The audio modality gives trainers the opportunity to position content on the grand stage inside the learners' heads, in their theaters of the mind. In little time, for virtually no cost, you can transport your learners to any scene in the world. You can help them paint rich images of your content that are very personal. However, like any theater show, there's lots of hard work to do behind the scenes. And the work has to be done in a sequence that is efficient. In the next chapter, we explore the podcast work flow.

Planning Audio Content

In This Chapter
- Why do you need to set up administrative processes?
- How do you frame a clear learning objective for your audience?
- How do you structure your audio content?
- What should you keep in mind when writing audio scripts?

It's tempting to wing it when it comes to producing learning podcasts. If you're producing a podcast or piece of audio streamed from a learning management system, simply turn on the microphone, press record, and start talking. In reality, winging it will almost always lead to dull and lifeless audio. And it will take longer to produce.

Yes, some media professionals seem to pull it off. They're talk show hosts or media personalities trained to churn out engaging commentary, whose minds are 120 percent focused on their content. When they're not on a live microphone they're thinking about how they sound, mulling over how they'll say it, and even rehearsing lines in their head. They're not like learning professionals, who have to squeeze their audio production into a spare hour between designing classroom activities, creating presentation slides, and doing research.

Planning, not winging it, is what leads to professional sounding podcasts. It saves time from having less mistakes to correct. It allows you to get it right the first time and avoid having to ad-lib the same 45-second monologue over and over. It also gives you greater precision with the editorial direction through well-organized scripts and coherent interviews.

In some respects, the process of planning audio content has a lot in common with instructional design. However, instead of planning to keep a classroom lively and engaging, you're staging a learning experience in the theater of the learner's mind. And just as instructional design starts with learning objectives and clarifying who the learners are, good audio planning does too. Once you have your objective you break it into chunks, structure it, choose an audio format, script it, and then perform all those pesky admin tasks that will keep you out of trouble down the line.

In this chapter we're going to explore these tasks and consider how you can put them into action when you create audio learning content. We start with setting up some basic administrative processes.

Set Up Your Administration Processes

Good administrative habits are important, especially when the project is complex and you are working with multiple people. Before you start your project, build a folder structure to store documents and audio files so you and your team can find them easily when you need them. You might be able to get away with sloppy file management if you're producing a one-off audio piece or if you're working on your own. But as your project becomes more complex and other people are involved in the production, poor admin will cause confusion and slow things down.

You can manage your files in many ways, but what's important is to follow your system consistently. Here's a suggested file structure if you don't already have a system working for you. You can come up with your own folder names. Remember to create a folder for every series of podcasts and include the following subfolders:

- **Common Media:** Include theme music, jingles, or specially recorded sequences that will be used in every episode of a podcast series. (For example, a standard opening or closing sequence may feature a mix of spoken word, sound effects, and music.) Create a subfolder to keep copyright licenses for the music or effects, plus artist clearances if using a singer or voice-over artist.
- **Pan-Episode Content:** If you have content that will be used in more than one episode, file the originals here. It may be an interview that you are breaking into five parts, playing each part in another episode.
- **General Administration:** You need a folder to store general files related to podcasts such as running plans, templates, and responsibility maps.
- **Episode:** Create an individual folder for every episode. Include these sub folders:
  - **Raw Audio:** This is where you save raw audio that's been recorded specifically for this episode, such as interviews and monologues.
  - **Project File:** This is where you keep your project file. We'll talk more about project files when we talk about editing.
  - **Final Media:** This is where you keep your final rendered file.
  - **Admin:** This is for scripts, plans, and copyright clearances for music and sound effects that are specific to that episode.

Frame Your Learning Objective

The first task in planning audio content is to frame the learning objective, which provides clear direction as you start and acts as an editorial yardstick to ensure every element is relevant. Most learning professionals construct learning objectives in three parts, influenced by Robert Mager's (1962) work on criterion referenced instruction. First, the objective should describe what the learner will be able to do after the instruction, the condition under which it will be accomplished, and the standard of performance.

Let's say you are teaching someone to record an audio interview for a weekly learning podcast using a Tascam DR-05 digital audio recorder. The first component of the learning objective, what the learner will be able to do at the end of the instruction, is simply to record an interview with a Tascam DR-05. However, describing just the action itself is very broad. For example, will the audio be recorded in someone's office or at an external location such as a convention center? Both situations require a different set of skills because these are very different environments. For example, if you are recording at a convention center it's important to find a quiet space with no music or distracting noises in the background. This ensures audio clarity. And often, in public buildings, music is piped through PA systems, which can cause serious problems for editing the interview. Recording in an office presents a different set of dynamics. For example, are you standing or sitting? Where do you put the microphone? How do you deal with air conditioner noise?

By stating the condition in which the learner will perform this task, you can more quickly determine what to include in the instruction. For example, if teaching someone to record an interview in an office, it makes little sense to include instruction on the perils of background music when recording interviews because people tend not to have music piped into their office. Finally, what standard is expected? Is the standard a technical measurement, such as setting recording levels or judging appropriate mic proximity, or an editorial measure, such as the duration of the interview or the way questions are phrased?

The more specific your objective, the more focused your learning content will be because it will help you weed out content that is not relevant. There's much more to learning objectives, such as the domains of learning and Bloom's Taxonomy, but they are outside the scope of this book. The bottom line is don't start working on audio learning content until you have a learning objective.

Know Your Audience

It's also important to know who is doing the learning. This knowledge should influence how you construct your podcast, including everything from word choice to selection of analogies and how you present information. One way to understand your audience and remain mindful of this throughout production is to develop a persona. A persona is a fictional character you create to represent the life, interests, and behaviors of a typical member of your listening audience. It's like an avatar you visualize as you create content. The value of a persona is that this person stays in your mind as you write your script so you'll find yourself writing for this person, using her language, and choosing content you know will make sense to her.

When you develop a persona for your learner, consider things like generation, level of education, hobbies, aspirations, and fears. You can also create a persona board to post pictures of this typical learner. Keep it nearby to remind you about for whom you are producing the content. You can create a persona board by sifting through magazines or photo albums to find pictures of people who look representative of the average person in your target audience. If your target audience is midcareer professionals in their forties who are health conscious and technologically savvy, you might search for a picture of a woman in her 40s wearing yoga clothes using an iPad, and a picture of a man on a bicycle in athletic gear with a Bluetooth headset.

It's helpful to give your persona a name and post additional pictures onto your persona board of items and activities that are of likely interest. For example, maybe it's a picture of an aircraft if your target audience enjoys travel.

Visualize Your Listener

I was taught as a young broadcaster to picture someone in my mind whom I knew well and talk to that person when I was on the air. The idea behind this was that I would sound more personal and informal. One of my friends who produced educational radio in London for more than 20 years told me she would visualize her mother and talk to her whenever she was on the air and write scripts for her when she was preparing them. This helped her choose words that were easy for her mother, so anyone would understand them, and kept her from saying things that may not have been appropriate. Developing a persona can help you plan, write, and present to your audience and sound not only more personal, but also more relevant.

Break Down Your Learning Objective

Once you have your learning objective, it's time to break it down into digestible chunks of knowledge. This is a general process that applies to any modality. For example, if you are teaching your learners to use "I statements" in conflict resolution, you might break the learning into three chunks. They might be what an "I statement" is, why it helps to defuse conflict situations, and what practical steps the learners can take to use them. Before you consider whether to plan an interview, a role play, or a monologue, you need to be very clear about what is involved in performing the task you will be instructing them on.

If you're not sure where to start, you could consider using the Kipling Method. Popular with journalists, it asks the what, when, who, where, why, and how of the learning objective:

- What is the task?
- Where is it performed?
- Why is it necessary?

- When should the task be performed?
- Who performs the task?
- How do you approach the task?

Jotting down your answers to these questions—using sticky notes, one for each chunk of information—can help you play around with their sequence and see how they look when structured in different orders.

Alternatively, you could ask the following three questions:

- What does my learner need to *do* to be successful?
- What does my learner need to *know* to do this successfully?
- What *attitudes* does my learner need to perform this task successfully?

Structure Your Content

When you have broken your audio content into chunks, it's time to structure the audio package and determine how to present each element.

Instructional Structure

When instructional designers plan learning events, they want them to flow logically, be easy to understand, and include activities that ensure retention. These events need to include a clear overview that contextualizes the learning and explains to the learner why it's relevant. These elements are important for podcasts, too.

There are many creative ways to achieve this. One place to start is to adapt the ROPES model, used by instructional designers to block out face-to-face instructional events, and apply it to digital learning content. ROPES stands for five instructional components to include in a learning event:

- **Review.** The trainer starts by reviewing the learner's current knowledge and relating the objective to the learner's experiences. This gives the trainer an opportunity to gauge the learner's level of knowledge and make appropriate adjustments. It also enables the trainer to help the learner identify an appropriate memory with which to contextualize the new knowledge.
- **Overview.** Then the trainer provides a high-level summary of what participants will learn, which may include key steps in the course and a picture of what the participant will be able to do when she has finished the instruction.
- **Present.** Now the trainer presents each step of the course content in detail. In a classroom, the trainer will use many different learning methodologies, which could include things like a demonstration, discussion, game, or lecture. The trainer will also relate how each step fits into the overall picture.
- **Exercise.** This is where participants practice the new skill and either the trainer or a peer provides performance feedback. It's where they do most of their learning.

- **Summary.** Here either the trainer or learners summarize what they learned. This is important for consolidating the topic and also providing an opportunity to improve retention through rehearsal.

ROPES in its original form makes great sense for the classroom but doesn't immediately translate to the digital media context unless we tweak it a bit, in particular the *R* and *E* stages.

One of the purposes for reviewing existing knowledge in the R stage is for the trainer in a live environment to gauge the learner's existing knowledge and skills so he can adjust the pace or add or subtract content to be more learner-centered. However, this is not possible with digital media, in which the content is already produced; there's no way to immediately adjust content that has already been recorded. However, because learners make sense of what they learn through their memories, the review stage still provides a valuable opportunity to help the learner find an appropriate memory with which to make sense of the message and relate its value to her work, which makes it more personal.

The *E* stage of ROPES is crucial in a class setting. It's probably the most important phase of learning because this is where the learner embeds her learning by doing (rehearsal) and receiving feedback. However, it presents difficulties for digital learning content, especially in asynchronous situations where the learner accesses the content more or less on demand by herself, where there is generally no avenue for immediate feedback. So it becomes difficult to include the *E* in digital content. Therefore, for digital content, *ROPES* becomes *ROPS*.

If we were creating an audio podcast about how to use "I statements" following the ROPS model, it might look like this:

- **Review.** Challenge the listener to recall the last time he experienced conflict and consider how helpful it would be to have a strategy to deal with it. Then suggest he'll learn one with "I statements."
- **Overview.** Explain at a high level that he needs to know three things:
  - What "I statements" are.
  - Why "I statements" work.
  - How to apply "I statements."
- **Present.** Go into depth about each of the three points. Explain how each point will help him defuse conflict situations. For example, understanding what "I statements" are will help you use them to reduce conflict, structuring them correctly will reduce conflict, and so forth.
- **Summarize.** Now you go back and summarize each of the three points for reinforcement.

You can create your own template to follow that incorporates an overview, detail, and repetition, but ROPS is an easy place to start.

Audio Content Techniques

Now that you have a general structure for your audio package in place, it's time to consider which technique will be best to communicate your learning content. Many people instinctively turn on their microphone at this point and start talking. But that's not very engaging, especially when other techniques could make it more interesting. For example, a role-play demonstrating how to phrase "I statements" would be much more effective than a monologue, while an interview with someone who experienced conflict and then put "I statements" into practice may be more motivational.

Voice-Overs

Voice-overs add energy to your speech and offer variety from straight speech without music. A voice-over generally starts with a few seconds of music, which quickly fades under the presenter's voice. You can make your voice-overs sound tighter by fading the music quickly after a bar or so of music. If you let the music play on too long before it fades under your voice, the voice-over will lose energy. Also, don't wait for the music to totally fade before you start talking. This robs the voice-over of energy. Start your fade before the first beat of the second or third bar of music so that it has half faded when you start talking and then it continues for a second or so after you have started the voice-over. As you fade the music level under your voice, make sure you drop the volume sufficiently. Many people suffer degrees of hearing loss, which makes voice-overs difficult to understand when the music is too loud. As a rule of thumb, set your level of background music as soft as you can without making it impossible to hear.

Audio offers many ways to convey information. These include:

- **Monologue.** One person presents the information. It's like a talking essay and feels like a direct conversation with the listener. It can be powerful and feel personal.
- **Dialogue.** Two people perform a conversation on a topic. It's less personal than a monologue because the listener is an observer rather than a virtual participant. But it adds an extra voice, providing variety and change.
- **Interview.** A guest, usually a subject matter expert, answers a series of questions. Effective interviewers act as the listener's representative and set up the questions so the listener feels as if the guest is talking directly to her.
- **Panel Discussion.** Two or more people engage in a facilitated conversation about a topic. It's similar to a dialogue, except the conversation is kept on track by a facilitator. It provides diversity of opinion, but the listener is an observer and thus less engaged.

- **Vox Pops.** This is a sequence of short soundbites from everyday people expressing their opinion, also known as "man on the street interviews." Vox pops generally add gritty credibility and keep things interesting with different voices.
- **Role Play.** This is like an audio drama of either a fictitious example or a re-enactment of a real event. Role plays are powerful because they express relationship dynamics well and are intriguing.

Additional Thoughts

Once you have created the structure and determined what audio content techniques you will use in the podcast, you are well on your way. Here are a few other tips to ensure your audio content is engaging:

- Start your podcast with an upbeat music track to create energy.
- Keep monologues to less than three minutes. If you need more time for the topic, short music stings of less than 15 seconds are great ways to break up monologues, if used sparingly.
- Feature regular "recaps" to summarize key points.
- Mix up the formats. Go from an opening monologue to an interview, and then to a role play.
- Include multiple voices. Consider using two presenters.
- Create anticipation by regularly making reference to what's coming up in the podcast. Explain how it fits into what you've already discussed so far, as well as how it helps the learner.

Opening and Closing

Start and finish your audio content with a positive, upbeat feel. A short music track that sets the tempo then fades for a voice-over can do this for you. Be sure to give a reason in your intro why the learner should continue listening by describing the learning objective and explaining the "what's in it for me." When you finish, summarize the content and remind learners why what they learned from the audio content is important.

Write Your Script

It can be tempting to avoid writing a script. It may seem cumbersome and time-consuming. However, a script helps in many ways. It will ensure that you use the correct words and phrases, particularly important when discussing potentially sensitive legal issues or narrating a branding message. A script will help you sound more confident, omitting uncomfortable pauses when you stop the flow to search for the next word or phrase and strengthening your authority. Likewise, a script will help you make fewer mistakes, saving you from rerecording your script multiple times or doing extensive edits. And a script will allow you to be more polished and engaging, freeing your brain to focus on vocal dynamics, not word choice and sentence construction.

You may have heard some people suggest that a script makes them sound unnatural. More often than not, they sound unnatural because the scripts were poorly written. Almost a century of radio broadcasting has enabled broadcasters to hone the way they write for the ear and develop a set of conventions that will make the presenter sound better. Let's explore these conventions and apply them to digital learning content by looking at four areas of writing for the ear:

- tone
- word choice
- sentence structure
- quotations.

While these directly apply to audio writing, they also apply to writing video scripts with one important difference, which we'll discuss in chapter 10.

How Is Your Learner Listening?

Think about where your learners are listening and what device they are using. This can influence the length of your audio content, its production feel, and its topic. For example, if they're listening at home, they're likely to have more space to sit and concentrate with fewer distractions. However, if they're on the road waiting for a plane or train, they might prefer to grab nanolearning chunks. You might also consider less music and fewer sound effects for learners on the run because there are more audio distractions to compete with. Use your knowledge of where people mostly listen to the audio to make references that are relevant to where they are. For example, if your learners listen while driving the car, make references to traffic. If they're in the office, use references like the water cooler or getting through security. Be conscious of their here and now.

Tone

Write your scripts in a conversational tone. Formal language tends to be wordy and takes your listener's brain more time and effort to process. And because audio is an immediate and relational modality, listeners feel as if you are talking directly to them and might be put off by stuffy language.

Adopt a one-to-one approach. Don't say, "My audience might find it interesting to . . ." because this suggests your listener is just one person in a large crowd. Instead say, "You might find it interesting . . ." Audio is personal and singular, not aloof and plural. Each listener should believe he is the only person you are talking to.

Word Choice

Words are tools to build understanding. The best are quick and easy to understand. Here are some tips on word choice when writing an audio script:

- Choose short words, especially monosyllables. *End* is better than *conclusion*, and *start* is better than *commence*.
- Opt for simple rather than complex words. *Equal* is better than *commensurate*, and *carry out* is better than *implement*.
- Use concrete words rather than abstract words. *Radial saw* is better than *tool*, and *Toyota Prius* is better than *hybrid*.
- Choose words that are easy to pronounce. *Weather bureau* is better than *bureau of meteorology*; same with *it is a concern*, rather than *it is worrisome*.
- Consider words that sound like their meaning, a concept known as onomatopoeia. *Thump* and *whoosh* work well.
- Opt for words that sound good, such as those that end with strong consonants. *Stop* is better than *pause*.
- Use familiar words and avoid technical jargon or verbose words. *Increase the size* is better than *upsize*. *We're aiming to buy the companies that supply our goods* is better than *we're aiming for vertical integration*.

Sentence Structure

Long sentences force your listener to do more work to decode your message than shorter sentences. So keep your sentences short. Here are five ways to keep your sentences short and dynamic:

- Cut redundant words. Review each sentence with a red pen and delete any word that does not add meaning. Be ruthless.
- Write in the active voice. This means you put the actor before the action in each sentence. For example, "The book on vintage cars was written by Ed Smith," is passive voice because the actor, Ed, comes after the action of the book being written. When expressed in the active voice it is more direct and has fewer words: "Ed wrote the book on vintage cars."
- Write one-clause sentences. The clause is the basic unit of a sentence and contains a subject and verb: "John bought an iPad." Some clauses, known as independent clauses, exist on their own. Others, known as dependent clauses, need another clause to make sense. So the clause "who just got a raise" makes no sense on its own and depends on another clause to make sense, such as the clause, "John bought an iPad." The written word is much more interesting when we combine clauses such as, "John, who just got a raise, bought an iPad." However, this is harder to hear as audio and decode. Therefore, if

you have sentences for your audio script like this with a dependent clause, make it two sentences: "John got a raise. So he bought an iPad."

- Read your script out loud and listen to how the words sound together. A radio news bulletin once ran with the headline, "Concerns over attacks on senior citizens." When you read that out loud it could sound like "a tax" on senior citizens. We need to check all our sentences. I was at an event where a boss was talking about his staff and he said, "Our colleagues have been doing some amazing things." Unfortunately his accent made it sound like, "Alcoholics have been doing some amazing things," which I'm sure is also true, if not what he meant.
- Paraphrase direct quotes. A direct quote is where the podcaster reads out what someone else said, word for word. Direct quotes always sound synthetic and you end up being an actor: "Bill Strong said, 'I don't like to eat ice cream in the winter.'" Instead, paraphrase the quote: "Bill Strong doesn't like to eat ice cream in the winter." Of course it would be even better to use a recording of Bill Strong saying it himself.

Script Mechanics

Your script should be as easy to read as possible. You don't want to lose your place in the middle of recording a monologue and have to start again simply because the lines on your script were too close together or the column width too wide. Here are some things you can do to make your scripts easy to read when performing them:

- Set your page so the column is 10 or fewer words. Wide columns—15 to 20 words— make it difficult for your eye to find the next line.
- Allow yourself a wide margin. More white space makes it feel less cluttered and gives you space to scribble down last minute notes in the margin.
- Use a serif typeface for scripts printed on paper and sans serif font if you are reading off a screen. Use both upper and lower case letters so it's easier to recognize words. However, if it's something you need to read more carefully, such as a name, do it in capitals because your eye will take more care to read it.
- Don't run paragraphs or sentences over two pages if printing on paper. If you need to turn over the page, plan it for the end of a sentence, when there is a natural pause.

Copyright and Permissions

An important part of planning audio content is clearing copyright for music and other intellectual property you will feature. Note that this is not a legal primer on copyright. But you should remember some basics.

Anything you create is your own intellectual property, unless you assign your rights to someone else. If you compose an original song or write an original poem, you own it and have the right to charge a fee to anyone who wants to use it. Likewise, if you want to use music in your podcast or audio learning content that someone else wrote, performed, and published, that person has the right to charge you for it. If you use a song by Beyoncé in your podcast, you need her permission, and if she's like most artists who live off their royalties, she'll charge you for it. You'll also need the permission of the person who wrote the song and the record label.

This makes commercial music quite complex if you want to use it in your podcast. Instead, you are better off finding production music that is written specifically for radio, television, cinema, podcasts, online video, and games. Production-music companies, sometimes referred to as royalty-free music providers, provide libraries of music categorized into genre, style, mood, and others that you can license. Usually, each specific piece of music will be offered in multiple lengths. Sometimes, they will have different versions, such as a melodic version or just a rhythmic version.

What about nonmusic content and copyright? If you're interviewing subject matter experts, it's a good idea to get them to send you an email that says they agree to be part of your audio content or create a form they can sign. If they are being interviewed, they likely have done so as a matter of consent. However, if you plan to use that content commercially, such as in a publicly sold training program, you should have their signature to show that they allow that.

Summary

Before you pick up a microphone or hit record, it's important to carefully plan both the content of your audio and the production process:

1. Create a folder structure for your project.
2. Start with a clearly defined learning objective.
3. Know your audience.
4. Break learning down into chunks.
5. Create a structure for your learning, such as ROPS.
6. Write your script.

Your Audio Toolkit

In This Chapter
- What are the essential tools of audio production?
- What are the optional tools of audio production?
- What environment is best to record in?

When most people walk into a new house, they don't ask whether the carpenter used a nail gun or hammer, whether the power saw came from The Home Depot or Harbor Freight, or whether the builder wore gloves when installing the drywall. They just care that the house is safe, looks good, and is functional. They take in the aesthetics and functionality of the house.

Consumers and audio content aren't all that different. They don't care whether you used a digital recorder to record a monologue or the audio app on your iPhone. They just want to listen to your content and learn.

This chapter will explore the tools of audio you need to produce audio content—not the fanciest, most expensive toys, but the gear that allows you to make good content without breaking the bank. It will start with the "must-have" audio tools, the core tools of the trade. Then it will dive into the "nice to haves" that give you more creative options to create engaging content.

Essential Tools of Audio Production

Recording audio doesn't have to cost much. In fact, you can be up and running for under $100. You just need a microphone, something to record on, something to listen back to it with, and a space to do the recording.

Microphones

Choosing a microphone can be quite daunting when you see all the options. A quick search online might bring up hundreds of different makes and models. But the microphone is the heart of audio recording, so you need to make a good decision.

Not all microphones are alike. Different ones respond differently to different voices, so microphone choice can be very personal. In fact, some radio announcers actually bring their own microphone into the studio rather than use the one in the studio. If you buy a microphone in a shop, rather than from an online retailer, take some time to try out different models. Listen to them and choose one that makes you sound good.

Dynamic Versus Condenser

Your first purchase choice is between a dynamic or condenser microphone (Figure 6-1). Dynamic mics tend to be more robust than condensers, although condensers are more sensitive and pick up more detail in the higher audio frequencies.

Figure 6-1. Dynamic and Condenser Microphones

A dynamic microphone (left) is usually robust and does not need a
battery or external power. A condenser microphone (right) tends to be
more sensitive but requires a battery or external power.

A dynamic microphone uses a magnetic coil in the diaphragm to convert the sound waves, whereas the condenser microphone uses a capacitor. The capacitor in a condenser microphone requires electrical current to work, so it will need either a battery or external power supplied from a mixing desk or audio recorder, which is called "phantom power."

Some higher-end condenser microphones, like those used on video cameras or in recording studios, do not have a space for batteries and can only be used with devices that supply the phantom power. Be sure to check before you purchase if your mic requires phantom power and if your audio recording device or mixer can supply it.

USB Microphones

A recent development in microphone technology is the USB microphone. This is a plug-and-play device that you can connect to your laptop through the USB port. Most computers will detect the microphone and automatically configure it for use, making it a great trouble-free option. The downside to USB mics is that they tend to be less responsive than traditional mics, so you need to position the mic closer to your mouth. Another limitation is that many models also have a record-only function, so you can't listen to your voice while you record. And to play back your recording, you need to pull the USB microphone out of the computer.

Headset Mics

Some people use headset microphones to record podcasts. Marketed to gaming enthusiasts and people who make VoIP calls, they're relatively cheap and may seem like a good option. Some even come with noise reduction to help reduce background noise. However, unless you buy a studio-quality model, which are often quite expensive, the audio quality of headset mics is usually very poor. The noise reduction feature is not as effective as one would hope and the frequency response may make you sound like you're talking on a telephone. They also pick up a lot of breathing because they're positioned awkwardly relative to the mouth. I have nothing against headset mics when used in gaming and for VoIP. But the purpose of microphones when recording podcasts is to reproduce the voice and other sounds so they are realistic. And for you to sound real and natural in your podcast, most headset mics will not cut it. For another $15, you can dramatically improve the audio quality with a better microphone.

Pickup Pattern

When you have chosen between a dynamic or condenser microphone, you need to consider its pickup pattern, also referred to as its polarity. The pickup pattern is the physical space around the microphone where the diaphragm is most sensitive, so that's where it will pick up sounds.

Omnidirectional microphones pick up sounds all around the head of the microphone. Cardioid microphones mostly pick up sounds in front of the head, while sounds behind it will either be very soft or not heard at all. This pattern is called cardioid because the polarity is shaped like an upside down heart.

Cardioid microphones have a number of variations. The most common is the hyper-cardioid pattern, which belongs to the long cylindrical microphones often referred to as shotgun mics. Shotguns are more sensitive to sounds in front of the microphone barrel and less sensitive to sounds to its side. Shotguns are used frequently with video cameras.

Balanced Versus Unbalanced

Media professionals often say they prefer balanced microphones because they don't pick up interference. Believe it or not, a standard audio cable can act as an aerial to pick up the buzz you hear in overhead lights, the hum from nearby electrical devices such as transformers, and even radio frequencies. These cables are known as unbalanced and have two wires to carry the audio signals. To overcome this, premium cables are given a third wire, which acts as a ground to reduce this interference. This is called a balanced cable. Balanced cables need a special plug called an XLR plug, which has three pins.

An unbalanced cable that is longer than 10 feet is more susceptible to interference and becomes more vulnerable the longer it is. So opt for balanced cables when your microphone is a long way from your recording device. Not surprisingly, balanced microphones are more expensive than unbalanced.

Accessories

Like any modern-day product, microphones come with accessories, which aren't necessarily upsells because they will help you sound better. One important accessory is a windscreen. This is a foam sleeve that fits over the microphone's head to reduce noise from wind, breathing, and to an extent, the air conditioner. It also helps reduce plosives, those little pops you hear on microphones when people speak the letters P and B.

If you are going to sit at a desk to record your audio, you should buy a microphone stand, which doesn't have to be expensive. If you buy one, make sure it comes with a microphone clip to hold the mic, which screws into the base. Clips are often included with microphones you buy and are not expensive. If you are using a studio condenser, you'll need both a stand and a shockmount.

A shockmount is a device that screws onto your microphone stand and holds the microphone in an isolated grip of rubber cables to isolate the mic from picking up noise, such as bumping the microphone stand or desk. In reality, noises will still be audible, just not as distracting. Another option is a two section broadcast arm that clamps onto your desk.

What Mic Should I Buy?

Every situation is different and you will, over time, determine from experience what microphone is best for you. However, if you're starting out, here are some recommendations. If you're planning to record a podcast in a fixed location, like at your desk, buy a studio condenser microphone with a large diaphragm. This will bring the best out in your voice. If you plan to hit the road and interview folks on location, buy a dynamic microphone with a cardioid pattern. And unless your microphone will be more than 10 feet away from your recording device, save some money and use an unbalanced microphone.

Choosing a good microphone is important to ensure you are clear in your recordings and sound natural as you convey learning. Poor-quality microphones can make some words difficult to understand and distract learners from your content.

Recording Devices

Once you have your microphone you need a device to record on. Very likely it will be your personal computer or a mobile device such as a smartphone, tablet, or digital audio recorder. This device will need audio editing software or an audio editing app.

Personal Computer

Most computers these days are equipped with acceptable quality sound cards so you can easily plug your microphone into the computer. Generally, the mic input will take a mini phono plug, so you'll need an unbalanced microphone. If you have a balanced microphone, you will need to buy a cable connector that converts it to an unbalanced signal. You can also use a plug-and-play USB microphone.

Your computer will need software to record and edit the audio. You can record with your PC using Microsoft Sound Recorder or on the Mac with Quicktime. However, a dedicated audio editing software package is better than just a voice recorder. There are a lot of audio editing software packages available. They include the open source software Audacity, and commercially available products like Sony Sound Forge, Avid Pro Tools, Adobe Audition, and the recently launched Hindenburg.

Editing software enables you to cut parts of your audio out and manipulate them. For example, if you make a mistake, you can edit it out or rearrange its order. Most editing software also provides tools to process the audio, such as graphic equalization and audio compression.

Embedded Recording Apps

Everyday portable devices such as smartphones or tablets offer apps to record audio. They are increasingly being used for newsgathering by major media companies because they're so portable and enable you to capture both audio and video in the same device. They also save you the cost of buying a separate device to record on, given everyone these days has a phone. They would be equally effective for the learning professional who might not have the budget to purchase a separate recording device.

The microphones built into phones are generally not located in a place that will get the best sound and are often poor quality, so it is worth buying an external microphone. However, beware that smartphones use different mic inputs from traditional recording devices, so you will need a mic that has a plug designed for phones and tablets. Smartphone mics have three rings on the tip of the plug, rather than the traditional two. You also have the option of USB mics, which tend to be pricey, and Bluetooth devices. At the end of the day, it doesn't really matter if you use a phone plug, USB, or Bluetooth mic. The important choice is to avoid using the built-in mic and get one that gives you more control to get better audio.

There are many apps for both iPhone and Android that provide both recording and editing functions. It's risky to list them here because the products change and are added to weekly. However, here are a few to explore, and don't forget to look into new options as they are launched. For Androids, try Lexis Audio Editor and Voice Pro—HQ Audio Editor. For iPhone and iPad, try the Hindenburg Field Recorder and Spreaker Studio.

Headphones or Speakers

Ultimately, you need to hear what you are recording and editing. This means acquiring either a set of headphones or loud speakers.

When choosing your headphones, look for a pair that will be comfortable on your head. It only takes half an hour before a cheap pair can start feeling tight, placing pressure around the head. While earmuffs might be good for isolating some external noise, they can cause you to sweat around the ears, presenting hygiene issues if you share them. (Many broadcasters bring their own headphones, rather than use the communal set left in the studio.) A good pair of affordable headphones can cost around $90, but you can find entry-level studio headphones for $30.

Figure 6-2. Pair of Headphones

Headphones are critical for monitoring the audio you are recording.
Look for sets that are comfortable to wear.

If you're considering loud speakers for your desk, look for a set of near-field monitor speakers. These are designed to be placed equidistant from you and each other so that you and the speakers form an equidistant triangle. This enables optimum stereo separation. You also need to check whether the speakers are active or passive. Active speakers have an amplifier built into them, so you simply connect a cable from your computer to them. Passive speakers need an amplifier, which will be an additional expense.

Optional Tools of Audio Production

What if the learning department has a little extra money in its budget? Here are four devices to expand your opportunities for more creative audio content creation.

Digital Audio Recorder

If you plan to record your own sound effects or interview subject matter experts, you'll need a portable digital audio recorder. This is the modern-day equivalent of the portable cassette recorder that journalists used to sling over their shoulders. Today's devices, the good and affordable ones, range from $80 to $250 and produce better audio quality than professional cassette recorders did 20 years ago.

What do you look for in a portable digital recorder? It should be able to record in WAV or MP3 format. WAV is the professional production standard and is preferable to MP3. Don't make the mistake of buying a traditional Dictaphone, which will likely have a lousy mic and record in a nonstandard format.

Buy a simple digital recorder. Many on the market today are designed for musicians, so they offer more features than you will need for interviews and sound effects. For example, a high-tech recorder might record on four tracks; however, if you're doing a voice interview, you only need one track. If you're recording sound effects, you will need two tracks to create stereo separation. Having four tracks is an unnecessary layer of complexity. Look for devices that record onto SD cards so you can easily transfer the audio file into your computer. Some devices are rechargeable, but it is more flexible to use normal batteries such as AA.

If you plan to interview SMEs for your learning content on location, you should consider buying a reporter microphone. A dynamic microphone, positioned six to 10 inches from your subject matter expert's mouth, will ensure even better quality sound than the digital audio recorder's built-in mics. Look for what is called a reporter microphone or an interview microphone.

USB Mixer

If you plan to conduct panel discussions with several people, you'll need multiple microphones, preferably one microphone for each panel member. You'll need to mix these microphones into one feed that connects to your recording device. This is done by a mixer (Figure 6-3).

You can buy a traditional mixer that simply provides one audio line out, which you can connect to your computer with a mini phone plug. However, you may find a USB mixer more convenient. It is a plug-and-play device, so you don't need to worry about setting up output levels from the mixer or working out a recording volume on your computer. Check whether your mixer provides phantom power to condenser microphones.

Figure 6-3. Audio Mixer

A mixer enables you to run several microphones at a time, which is
ideal when recording panel discussions or interviews.

Telephone Recorder

You won't always be able to go on location to interview SMEs, so you may need to use the telephone.
There are many ways to do this. One way is to use a telephone hybrid, which connects to both your
telephone and the device you will record on. This device separates out the incoming and outgoing
audio so they are distinct feeds, eliminating the annoying feedback loop. The advantage of a hybrid
is that while your interviewee will sound like he is talking to you over the phone, your voice will
come through a traditional microphone and your voice will be studio quality. Professional systems,
used by radio stations, cost thousands of dollars, while entry-level systems are about $500. You can
also use devices called telephone taps for less than $100, but these are clumsy to operate. Telephone
hybrids connect to mixers, so you could have someone on the telephone join a panel discussion.

If you have Skype, you can use your account to call landline phone numbers for a fee and use
software such as Pamela, MP3 Skype Recorder, or MX Skype Recorder. MX Skype Recorder will
integrate with Google Talk and other VoIP applications if you prefer to record your interview using
a different VoIP provider. You can also record interviews with your cell phone. Many free apps offer
this function, including Automatic Call Recorder, Super Call Recorder, and Andro Record for
Android, and Call Recorder, Call Log Pro, and ipadio for iOS.

Recording Environment

If you are in the position to create a dedicated space for recording, you will want your acoustics to
sound good. This means a room with no distracting noises and one where your voice does not echo.
Professional studios are designed to be soundproof and reduce echo. Soundproofing is very difficult and expensive. An easier problem to solve is reducing echo. Microphones record sounds that
bounce back and forth off reflective surfaces as echo. Rooms with a lot of echo are described as "live"
acoustic environments and generally have a number of surfaces, such as walls, that are parallel. If you

have the luxury of a dedicated space to record, aim for a room that has nonparallel walls or objects that absorb the sound, like heavy curtains or cloth chairs. Avoid rooms with tile or wood floors. You can also invest in acoustic tiles, which both absorb and reflect sound. If you don't have a permanent room, look to record in rooms with curtains, carpets, and walls that are at an angle.

If you can't afford a designated recording studio, consider an acoustic booth. This is like a soundproofed telephone box with acoustic tiles. Another option is an Acoustic Shield, also known as a reflective filter, which is a semicircular piece of stainless steel and acoustic foam between two and three feet wide that wraps around your microphone to reduce environmental noise and echo (note that it doesn't eliminate them). It can be mounted on your microphone stand and is highly effective at reducing the echo.

Summary

Learners tuning in to your podcast don't really care about what equipment you use to produce the audio. They're not asking, "Is it a cardioid microphone or a condenser?" They just want the podcast recorded in a way that makes it clear and easy to understand. So don't get too hung up on whether you buy the right brand of equipment. Just make sure it provides the functionality you need for crisp, clear audio. Think carefully about the microphone you buy and test it before making a decision to be sure it's right for your voice. Avoid headset microphones at all cost, and opt for simple digital recorders rather than ones with lots of fancy features. There's no need to spend a lot of money to build a good-quality audio toolkit because good-quality gear is quite affordable. With very simple and economic gear, you can produce excellent audio. Now that we've talked about the equipment you need, let's look at how to use it.

Creating Digital Audio Content

In This Chapter

- How do you record audio?
- How can you improve your vocal presence?
- What's the best method to conduct an audio interview?

Now that you've got your audio toolkit, it's time to use it. We started the last chapter talking about a house. When people walk into a house for the first time, they take in the design and tend not to spend much time looking at the crown molding or looking to see if the drywall was installed well. However, if there are lumps in the drywall or the crown molding is lopsided, it sticks out like a sore thumb.

The same applies to digital content. Listeners don't notice recording levels unless they're either too low or too high. They don't notice microphone proximity unless your mic is too close to your mouth or too far away. They tend to notice more of what goes wrong than what goes right.

In this chapter we're going to look at recording audio so the technique is invisible and your listeners are focused on the learning. We're going to run through some techniques to help with microphone technique and vocal presence. Then we'll look at conducting a professional-sounding interview in person and over the phone. But first, we're going to discuss using digital audio.

Understanding Digital Audio

Today, audio is produced as a digital signal. But 20 years ago it was recorded as an analogue signal on media such as reel-to-reel tapes, cassettes, cartridges, and vinyl records. The technical difference between analogue and digital is that analogue audio matches the sound, hence the term analogue. Digital audio records the sound in digital code. The practical difference, more importantly, is that digital audio tends to be nice and crisp when properly recorded and does not have the low hiss of magnetic tape or rumble from the turntable when playing a record.

Editing software packages visually display the audio as a waveform. Figure 7-1 shows the waveform as displayed in the audio editing software Audacity version 2.1.2. Each sound, whether it be a word or the sound of a door closing, appears as a series of waves. In reality, they simply look like a blob. The longer the duration of the sound, the wider the wave appears. The louder the sound, the larger it appears vertically. Silence is represented by a thin line running through the middle.

Figure 7-1. Sample Waveform in Audacity

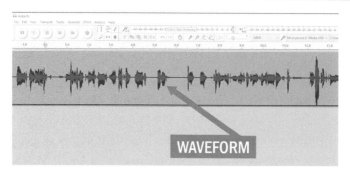

Audio can be recorded in multiple file formats. The most common formats are WAV and MP3. As a general rule, you should record original audio using WAV format and provide final copies that are being downloaded as MP3 files. WAV is the industry standard file format for audio production. It offers high-fidelity audio but is uncompressed, which results in large file sizes. MP3 files are compressed audio files and are a fraction of the size of the WAV files. Most music and podcast files you buy and download are MP3 files.

As you record audio, you need to monitor audio levels using peak program meters (PPM). These are the small meters that flicker whenever you are recording sound. PPMs measure the audio level up to 0 decibels (db). When the levels hit 0 db, the audio becomes distorted, also known as clipping. When the levels are too low, noise from the equipment, such as a hum, may be evident and qualities from the sound can be lost, which are hard to recover.

It is good practice to turn the audio level as high as you can, without it being high enough to clip. You can do this by conducting a test recording and watching the levels. If you're interviewing a subject matter expert, ask her to say a few words into the microphone and watch the PPMs. Generally, if they average at about -12 to -10 db you'll be fine. It's OK if they occasionally get close to 0 db for very short periods of time.

Most digital audio recorders offer automatic level control (ALC). This is where a chip in your digital recorder automatically adjusts the audio level to achieve its optimum level. This feature also exists in video cameras, which we will discuss in chapter 12. While it is best to manually adjust your levels, ALC in most digital recorders works fine.

Editing Audio With Audacity

It doesn't matter what editing program or app you use to make audio. What matters is the craft of editing. When I started in radio, I used a razorblade and editing block and literally cut reels of tape and then joined them back. Now we do it digitally on the computer. At the end of the day, your learner doesn't care how you edit or what software you use. I take an agnostic approach to software—it all has its pros and cons. You simply need to find one that suits your work style. In this book, I have chosen to demonstrate editing using Audacity, which is a free editing package you can download from the Internet. Audacity works both on Windows and Mac and offers everything you will need to create engaging learning audio content. The screenshots we use in this book are from the Windows version of Audacity, which is similar to the Mac version.

Recording Audio

Recording audio is relatively easy. You may record using your computer, a digital audio recorder, or a mobile app.

If you are recording on your computer you will most likely use audio editing software, such as Audacity, Microsoft Sound Recorder, or QuickTime. Recording on editing software is similar in most programs, although the buttons may look different or be placed in different parts of the screen. In Audacity, it's simply a matter of pressing the red record button. So to record audio, plug your microphone into the computer and make sure it works. Then open up the editing software and create a new project file.

Click the record button, wait for five seconds, then start talking. As you speak, you'll see the waveform of your speech appear on the screen. When you are finished, wait five seconds before clicking the stop button. You now have an audio track you can edit; the five seconds before and after provides breathing room for editing (see chapter 8 for more on editing audio). Once you have the track, save your project. It's a good idea to regularly save your work, even if your software is set to autosave.

Digital audio recorders tend to be fairly similar in layout, although each has its own set of nuances. It's like the differences between two different car models. They both have switches to turn on the lights, but they're in different places. You can find the controls quite quickly by playing around with the device or reading the user manual.

Most recorders have a record button and some have a separate stop button, while others require you to hit the record button a second time to stop the recording (Figure 7-2). With most recorders, once you start recording, the device creates a new audio file, automatically giving it a name. The name is usually a number such as "0003.wav." It can be easy to lose track of all the different files, so keep a log of each file name with a description. For example, "00.05.wav: interview with Freda Blogs on communication skills."

Figure 7-2. Sample Audio Editing Software

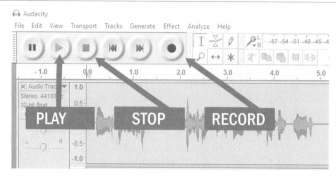

There are many audio recording apps available for both iPhone and Android. Many are designed to replicate the experience of a traditional digital audio recorder, while others simply offer record, play, and export. Some premium apps provide additional features such as editing and special effects like a graphics equalizer. Audio recording apps represent a very cost-effective way to record audio when you are on the go.

Sounding Professional

It's good to sound professional when you perform voice-overs or podcasts. Professionalism comes from using the microphone well, modulating your voice, and making technical adjustments to your recordings. We'll talk about the technical adjustments you can make that will improve vocal quality when we discuss audio editing in chapter 8. For now, we'll focus on how to use the microphone and what you can do to improve vocal dynamics.

Choose the Mic That Suits You, Not the One You Like

More than two decades ago I worked for a radio station that had a beautiful, high-end microphone worth $1,000. I loved using it because some of my colleagues sounded great on it. One day my boss came in and told me he didn't like the sound of my voice. "It feels muffled, not quite sharp," he said. So he got the technician in and we tried a bunch of different microphones. One mic, worth about $200, made my voice sound rich, crisp, and warm. From then on I did my show with that microphone, even though I loved that $1,000 one.

Microphone Technique

Every microphone is as different as is everyone's voice. This makes the way you use your microphone somewhat personal. Positioned near the corner of your mouth, one microphone may make your voice sound warm but cause another person's voice to feel cold and aloof. When using a microphone, you need to explore how it sounds in different positions and use the one that makes your voice sound best. If you're recording someone else, you'll need to do this for that person too.

The microphone, metaphorically speaking, is your listener's ear. How you position it will affect how the listener relates to you or your presenter. If the mic is closer, your voice will be more intimate; further away, more formal. Music radio stations, especially on FM, position their announcers very close to the mic so they can talk softly, without projecting their voices. This makes them sound like your friend. News stations will position their announcers farther back to project more authority. Think about how you want to sound and adjust the microphone position accordingly. A natural distance for most microphones is five fingers away from the mouth.

If you want your voice to sound warmer, you can take advantage of what's known as the Proximity Effect. As you move the microphone closer to the mouth, the warmer bass frequencies become exaggerated, giving you a richer tone. This works with most mics but not omnidirectional ones.

Plosives are a common problem that comes from the way a microphone is used. Plosives are sounds formed by the letters *P, B,* and others that create a popping noise on the microphone, which distracts listeners. To form these sounds, you must close your mouth and force a burst of air from your mouth that pops the lips open. You can feel this burst of air by putting your hand in front of your mouth and saying *P.* Try it. Feel the burst of air? Well, every time you say a *P* or *B,* this burst of air hits the microphone's diaphragm, temporarily overloading it, creating that annoying pop sound. You can reduce the effect of plosives by sticking your lower lip out farther than your upper lip so it absorbs some of the burst of air as you say these consonants gently. Another approach is to speak across the microphone at a 45-degree angle so the air burst passes the diaphragm.

Vocal Presence

Like mic technique, the best way to improve your vocal presence is to practice. Vocal presence is the product of how you use your voice. When you speak, your breath passes over your vocal cords, which are located in the voice box at the top of your windpipe. This creates a buzzing sound, which is then shaped by your throat and nose. It's here you get those lovely tonal qualities that makes your voice distinct from other people's. It then travels into your mouth, where your tongue, soft palate, teeth, and lips shape the voice into words.

The voice is an amazing part of our anatomy. And just about everyone was born with a lovely, rich voice. But over the years they learn how not to use it. People adopt poor posture because they're tired, stressed, or stuck in front of a computer all day, which stops them taking those lovely deep breaths that give their voice strength and presence. And they stop opening their mouth so words start slurring and are poorly formed.

If you want to improve your vocal presence, consciously work on your breathing, which will increase your voice's warmth and authority. Focus on how you use your mouth to shape words, which will make you sound more credible. And consider how you vary your delivery to sound more expressive, which will draw your learner in. If you struggle to improve your vocal presence, find a vocal coach with experience in voice-overs or radio work who can help you enhance your technique. If you can't find someone with voice-over experience, a singing teacher can help you understand vocal dynamics.

Breathing

It's important to breathe deeply to allow a full flow of air over the vocal cords. This will give you greater vocal strength while relaxing the throat, where your voice is formed. It's important to allow your ribcage to expand as you breathe in because this lowers the diaphragm, allowing deeper breaths. Sit or stand so your spine is straight but relaxed. If you are slumped you won't be able to breathe as deeply, reducing your capacity for air, which leads to a weaker voice.

What does all this mean in practice? First, relax. Roll your shoulders to release tension and then sit or stand straight. You don't need to be rigid—just comfortably straight. If necessary, massage your neck muscles. Now, take two or three nice deep breaths and allow the air to flow over your vocal cords. Take note of how it feels. Now, allow your breath to carry your voice to the front of the mouth. You'll notice that your vocal register is lower and your voice sounds fuller.

Enunciation

Good enunciation improves credibility. Native English speakers shape vowels and consonants at the front of the mouth. Vowel sounds are made by opening and shaping the whole of your mouth, while consonants are formed with your lips and teeth.

To improve your credibility, shape each word carefully and allow each consonant and vowel to be fully formed. It does not sound good to slur them or run them together. Most of the time this will not be a problem, but sometimes you'll stumble on tricky words that are hard to pronounce. Focus on these words with practice.

To practice a troublesome word, break it into its syllables and say the word slowly, carefully enunciating each syllable. For example, it's easy to pronounce *cognizant* as *connizant* and miss the *g*. So say it slowly a few times as *cog-ni-zant*, then start saying it a little faster, then faster, and speed it up until you are saying it at a natural speed.

Listen to how you speak and identify words you can enunciate more clearly. For example, *million* is often mispronounced as *mill-yon* and *Australia* is often mispronounced as *oz-tray-lya*. They should be pronounced *mil-li-on* and *Aust-ray-li-a*. We all have words we can sharpen up, so train your ear to recognize and practice them. Clearly enunciated words are easier for your listener to recognize.

People often debate how fast or slow you should speak. Should you deliver 140 words per minute or 180? There's no perfect answer to this because it depends on your personality and diction. Some naturally fast talkers who average 180 words a minute will sound contrived if they deliver 140 words per minute. And slow talkers will find themselves tripping over words if they increase their delivery speed. As a general rule, speak at the speed you feel most comfortable. If you find yourself tripping over your words, this is a sign you should slow down. If your listeners tell you they don't understand, that's another sign you should slow down.

Expression

If your delivery is dull and boring, listeners will zone out. One of the universal content principles is to keep changing elements of our content so the listener thinks he is missing something. One way to do this is regularly changing the dynamics of your voice. Here are five ways to do that:

1. **Pace:** You can affect energy levels by speeding up and slowing down. Speeding up increases excitement, while slowing calms things down.
2. **Pause:** Pausing before or after keywords, and sometimes before *and* after, can focus the listener's attention. If the listener has zoned out and you pause, it breaks the rhythm and he thinks he is missing something.
3. **Pitch:** Raising and lowering the pitch can increase or decrease emotional intensity. Lowering it calms it down. Pitch can be tricky because increasing pitch can indicate nervousness, so use it carefully.
4. **Power:** You can grab the listener's attention by increasing or decreasing your voice's power. If your listener has zoned out and you suddenly speak louder or softer, it draws him back. Dropping the power of your voice is more effective than increasing it.
5. **Repetition:** You can highlight certain words by repeating them. Not only does it grab attention, but it leads to better retention.

It's important to use these techniques subtly and weave them into your delivery in a way that doesn't draw attention to your technique. If it's obvious you're using a technique for the sake of using a technique, it loses its effect. Vocal dynamics is an art broadcasters and singers have been practicing for many years. Improving your vocal presence requires practice and listening back to your voice. But it's worth the effort.

Coaching Others

If other people are presenting your podcast or voice-over, they may need coaching. If you don't have the budget to hire a voice coach and find yourself guiding them, start with their speed and help them find a comfortable pace. Nerves often prompt people to speak faster than they normally would. Get them breathing deeply and ensure they're relaxed. Are they sitting or standing straight? If they trip over words, ask them to practice the troublesome words slowly, syllable by syllable. If they're sounding dull, get them to try one of the expression techniques just covered. Don't overload them with lots to work on all at once; start small, and as they develop, get them to work on new techniques.

Conducting Interviews

One of the most exciting opportunities that podcasting brings to learning is being able to bring more SMEs into the learning environment. But conducting interviews well takes practice. Let's explore how you can use them to drive powerful learning and discuss techniques that boost learning and make you sound great.

There are generally two types of media interviews. We can call the first the personality interview and the second the factual interview. With personality interviews, the guest is invited onto a podcast to make the presenter look good to the listener. This is common on television and radio programs, where the interviewer often shares an opinion and really only uses the guest to validate it. These types of interviews are all about the interviewer. With factual interviews, the interviewer is a facilitator who more or less sets up the relationship so it is between the guest and the listener. She will ask questions of the guest, then step away and let the guest talk. She won't spend her time imposing her opinions on the guest or trying to prove her expertise to the listener. Her role is to keep the interview on track or keep it rolling if the guest loses momentum. For our purposes the factual interview is most appropriate for learning, so we're going to run through how to conduct a factual interview that sounds great.

You have three duties when conducting an interview:

1. Coach your guest.
2. Ask questions.
3. Present and sound good.

Field Interviews

A powerful way to create a sound picture in your listener's mind is to feature an interview with subject matter experts in their natural habitat. For example, if you're interviewing a traffic cop, it would be nice to have some traffic noise in the background. If you're talking to a teacher, some playground noise or classroom bustle behind the interview would add that extra authenticity. The problem with doing the interview in this environment is that you can't control how loud the background is. So interview your subject matter expert in a quiet space. Then take your digital audio recorder out onto the street or playground and record three or four minutes of ambient noise. When you get to the edit, you can place this ambient noise in the background, behind the interview, and adjust the volume so that it's loud enough to be heard but soft enough not to be a distraction.

Coach Your Guest

Many SMEs are unaccustomed to, even intimidated by, being interviewed with a microphone in their face and the recording rolling. It's pretty easy to hear when someone is nervous and it will distract the learner from the content. So your first job is to put your SME at ease. He needs to feel comfortable opening up. If he's stressed, distracted, or feeling threatened, you will not get strong answers.

Invest time in building rapport. Do this from the moment you set the interview up and work at it throughout the process. Be open about the general things you will ask so he can be comfortable about what to expect. However, do not give him a list of your questions in advance. You don't want him to feel caught off guard, but you also don't want to receive labored or rehearsed answers. It could also cause problems if you follow up a comment and start asking questions about something he thinks you didn't agree to ask about. In this case his answers may come across as defensive.

Before recording, ask him how he feels. Does he need water? Can you get him anything else to feel comfortable before starting the interview? Be conscious of your body language and use appropriate eye contact. Maintain an open posture. Lean comfortably toward him to signify interest and be sure you are both sitting or standing on the same level. Altogether, this can create positive energy that lightens his stress levels and leads to a better-sounding interview.

If your guest seems uncomfortable, perform a quick 90-second dry run and use it as an opportunity to offer advice or reassurances. Crack jokes and be self-deprecating. Be prepared to restate questions and ask him to respond again but slower if he goes too fast. The more comfortable your guest is, the more likely he will have the capacity to carefully think about and respond to your questions. You don't want you learner thinking, "Gee, he sounds awful," or "He's very defensive," or "He doesn't know what he's talking about." You want the interview to lead the learner directly to learning.

Ask Questions

The purpose of questions is to get answers your learner is interested in. The more focused they are, the stronger the responses will be from your interviewee and the clearer the responses will be for your learner. Always prepare your questions in advance—don't wing it. Preparation allows you to focus all your attention on listening to him and responding with follow-up questions. When you plan your interview, know what you want your guest to say, in a general sense. This means thinking carefully about specific points of interest your learner would want to glean from your guest. Knowing what the learner will want allows you to carefully frame questions to draw these things out. In a sense, the interviewer's job is to represent the listener.

Before the interview, prepare an opening comment and closing statement, plus four or five specific questions. The opening and closing comments should be written for the learner, not the interviewee. Read the opening statement when you start to set the feel of a formal interview and help focus your learner.

As a general rule, start with open questions that get the conversation flowing and then move to closed questions to wrap up. Open questions are great for exploring topics, while closed questions are good for wrapping things up or making points. For example, "What sort of practical steps can leaders take to listen more to their staff?" gets your SME talking, whereas, "Do you think leaders need to listen to their staff more?" gets a simple yes or no. If you want the SME to make a point that you leave hanging or that becomes a key moment in the interview, a closed question can be powerful. "So leaders need to listen more to their staff?" You ask. And he replies, "Yes. Much more." At which point you have a strong ending.

Keep your questions short and simple, and avoid asking two questions at once. For example: "What are the main triggers for fight and flight reaction, and what do you suggest one does to avoid them?" Your guest will most likely choose the one he is most comfortable with or intrigued by, answer it, and then forget the other. Instead ask, "What are the main triggers for fight and flight reaction?" Allow him to answer, then follow up with, "What do you suggest to avoid them?" Of course, this is much easier when you have prepared the questions and they're on a piece of paper in front of you.

An exciting part of well-facilitated interviews happens when the guest opens up a line of comment that was unexpected but still relevant. If you are well prepared, you will have the cognitive space to listen and reflect as he speaks. Make sure you are comfortable and listen. When he says something you did not anticipate, and it still achieves your purpose for the interview, follow up and have him expand.

Present and Sound Good

Your questions will be heard by the listener, so they need to be articulate, clear, and well presented. It's tempting to think, "I'll just redub my questions in when I get back to the office if I sound dumb." But recording your questions and dropping them in will sound fake and listeners will be able to tell that they were recorded at different times. The human voice is incredibly transparent. To start, your rhythm and intonation will sound different because you will not be in rapport with the SME. You'll speak at a different speed. And the background acoustics will be different. Believe it or not, this gives away a lot of interviews. This is why it's important to write a script for your introduction, wrap-up, and questions. It's OK if you don't read them word for word—you'll be the only person who knows. But being prepared means you'll sound better. Keep some back-up questions ready in case your guest doesn't hit all the points you hope to cover.

Your job as a factual interviewer is to put the spotlight on your guest, not yourself. Only ask questions when you need to and allow the guest to keep talking as long as he's on point. If he answers a question you planned to ask in his general response to another question, that's fine. Cross that question off your list. Don't feel rushed during the interview. If you're not sure what to ask, take a breath and think about it. If this creates an awkward silence, you can always edit it out later.

In a factual interview, the SME's opinion is the sole focus. It's not your role to share your thoughts—you can do that elsewhere. Nor is it your role to agree or disagree. However, to encourage your guest you will often find yourself making comments or using attending skills that inject value judgments into the interview. Instead, use nonverbal cues such as nodding to keep the interview moving along. If you're conducting an interview over the telephone, you can encourage the SME's commentary with neutral utterances such as "OK, so cognitive psychology was a response to behaviorism, what happens when . . . ?"

One final comment about presenting your interview: While your job is to stay out of the spotlight so the listener's mind is totally focused on what the subject matter expert is sharing, you're still in control. You will often find when conducting an interview that your guest literally reaches for your mic and tries to take it from you. This is most often because he is nervous and physically holding the microphone gives him a sense of control. Interestingly, whoever holds the microphone has the power to keep talking and stop and start. If you try to break in and redirect the flow of commentary while he clutches the mic, you'll find it is very difficult. It's one of those funny things that you discover during an interview experience. When your guest physically takes the microphone, you lose your sense of control and the power to direct the questions. So never let go of the microphone.

Danger of the Conversational Chat

Some people might think it's easier to skip preparing interviews and following all these rigid rules. Instead they'd prefer an informal conversation. Sure, a conversational approach sounds engaging, but it makes life harder when you edit your interview. You'll want to remove some comments but find you're laughing over his comments and it spills over into something that is important; if you cut it, it will sound very unnatural. You might also want to take some sound bites from the interview to use in other learning content. But you can't because you and your guest are talking at the same time. So while these rules may seem like a lot of work, they are designed to give you more options. Professional journalists are trained to use these techniques because they allow for much more flexibility in using their content.

Summary

Your goal in making a learning podcast is have the learners focused entirely on the message. If they notice your technique, they're not focusing on your message and you have failed. Normally, it is poor technique that draws the listener's attention, often just one or two minor things that could be prevented. It can seem like there are a lot of skills for learning professionals to learn if they are to create engaging podcasts. Each skill, whether it be setting the audio levels or asking the right questions in an interview, involves varying degrees of complexity. But all are easy to learn and perfect with practice. Start by developing one skill at a time and add to it gradually, and you'll soon find it comes easily. These skills are what will enable you to create an overall podcast that can draw your learners in and keep them engaged. They are the skills that fade into the background, like good drywall and crown molding, unless they are poorly executed.

Once you have created your audio recordings, it is time to edit them together into the final package your learner will listen to.

Editing Digital Audio Content

In This Chapter

- What is the art of audio editing?
- How do you edit and process digital audio?
- How do you go from editing to a complete podcast?

You've planned your podcast, structuring it around a learning objective and with a specific listener persona in mind. You've also recorded and collected audio elements such as monologues, interviews, and panel discussions. Now it's time to assemble these disparate parts into a complete learning podcast that you can publish and distribute to your learners. Welcome to audio editing.

Audio editing used to be a physically intensive process. You had to cut the bits of your audio that you didn't want out of the tape. You had to mark the specific location of that sentence on the tape with a grease pencil and then use a razor blade and cutting block to cut it out. After that, you had to join it back together using special sticky tape. Today the process is entirely digitalized. You locate the start and finish of segments you want to cut by looking at digital images of the waveform instead of marking it with a grease pencil.

Traditionally, editing was the process of cutting out unwanted material—such as mistakes, repeated words, or parts of an interview that went off track—from your audio. You might also break up an interview and change its order. In addition, you would edit music and sound effects.

Today, audio editing software does more than just cut audio. It offers functions not traditionally part of editing, such as adding special effects and creating multitrack packages. Audio editing is now more a process of creating digital packages by cutting and pasting elements of sound, adding effects to correct or improve sound, and mixing multiple audio elements together.

Well-edited audio does not sound as if it has been edited. Spoken word content flows like a natural conversation and edited music has no interruption to its beat or rhythm. Listeners should be unable to identify where words, phrases, or even large sections of an interview or monologue have been removed. The best way to achieve a natural flow is to rely on your ears and keep listening to your edits to be sure they flow smoothly. It can be tempting, once you get used to recognizing the shape of sounds appearing as waveforms, to simply use the visual representation of the waveform to identify where a sound starts and stops. But often it doesn't capture the natural breath and intonation of the speaker.

Editing audio, as well as video and text, raises a number of ethical issues. You have the power to change what someone appears to be saying and if your skills are well developed, no one will ever know. Political news media has landed itself in numerous controversies in which key elements of a soundbite were left on the cutting room floor, thus contributing to the rising level of distrust in modern journalism. In reaction to this, some have suggested news media—and by extension, learning professionals—should not edit interviews. This is a knee-jerk reaction: It was not the editing that was bad in these cases, but the ethics. When you edit, it's important to do so in a way that makes the content easier to understand without undermining its accuracy. As a general rule, you should also tell your interviewees they will be edited for brevity and relevance.

How do you decide what to cut from an interview and what to leave in? The answer is go back to your learning objective and determine whether the comment or sequence of comments in question leads the learner to the learning objective. If not, take it out. Good editors will ruthlessly cut material. But they won't make the decision based on whether they thought the comments were nice or right. They'll decide based on a clear understanding of the learning objective.

Let's walk through the editing process. First we'll look at cutting and splicing your audio—that's the traditional term for audio editing. Then we'll look at which effects can make your audio easier to hear. And we'll finish with multitracking. The good news is that digital audio editing is very easy to learn and with practice you can quickly improve your skills. If you know how to edit the written word using a word processor, you'll find editing audio easy and fun to learn.

Editing Audio

The technical process of audio editing is like editing a document in a word processor. You might read a sentence, select a word you think is redundant, and then delete it. Or you may cut and paste a sentence to another section of the document. When you edit audio, instead of selecting typed words, you are selecting a visual representation of the sound wave that was picked up in the recording and then deleting or cutting and pasting it. You'll remember from chapter 7 that digital audio appears in editing programs as a waveform. Each blob on the waveform is a sound that may be a word, sound effect, or piece of music. Silence is represented by a thin line.

Figure 8-1 shows what a sound waveform looks like in the freely available audio editing software Audacity.

Figure 8-1. Example of Waveform in Audio Editing Software

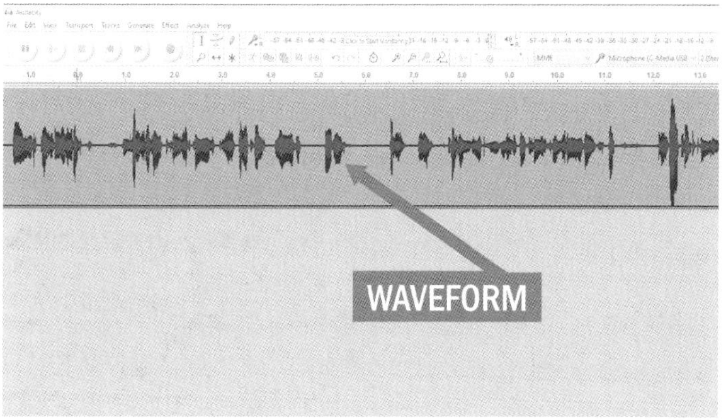

The waveform is a visual representation of the sound you are editing.

You will manipulate this waveform using a number of controls. But before you can use these mechanical controls, you need to select the mode. For editing, you need to be in selector mode.

It's important to familiarize yourself with the practical editing tools in your audio editing program. The most important ones are cut, copy, and paste. When editing, you will also need to use the zoom controls to zoom in and out of the waveform.

Once you have an understanding of the basic editing controls, it's now time to edit. To do so you need to listen to your audio and determine what to cut. Position your cursor at the beginning of the track and either hit the space bar or click on the play button. You'll see the cursor start moving to the right. As the cursor passes over the waveform, it will appear above the blob representing the sound you can hear. For example, when you hear the word *hello*, the cursor will be passing over the blob representing hello. If you hit the space bar again to stop playing, or use the stop button at the top of your screen, it will stop and the cursor will return to the position it started. If you want to remove the word *hello*, you will need to click your mouse over the blob representing it and the cursor will be positioned there (Figure 8-2).

Figure 8-2. Example Showing Selected Audio Segment

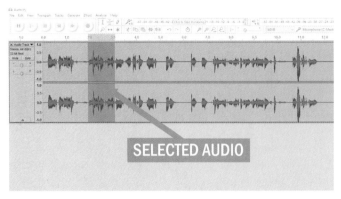

Editing audio involves manipulating elements of audio. To do this, you select the elements in much the same way as you select words in a word processing program.

With the blob selected, you can delete it by clicking on the scissor icon at the top of the screen. You can also cut or copy and paste it if you wish.

It is best to listen to what you're about to cut to ensure that you've selected the right element and cut all of it. You can listen by pressing the space bar or clicking on the play button at the top of the screen. You don't want to cut just the *-llo* part of *hello* and leave the *he-*. You want to remove the whole word. Cutting a word or sound in half makes it sound very unnatural and distracts the learner's attention away from the content. Once you have deleted your selection, play it back to make sure it sounds natural. If it doesn't, undo the edit and try again.

Your task in editing is to work your way through the whole interview, monologue, panel discussion, or role play and remove any audio that distracts from the objective.

Cut Out Anything That's Not Relevant

Highly disciplined editors are ruthless and cut as much out of interviews as possible. The shorter the better. Workshop attendees often cringe when I tell them this. They say they don't want to offend their subject matter expert who gave them a half hour interview by using only two minutes. But isn't it more offensive to the listener to drag him through half an hour of irrelevancies just because we don't want to offend the expert?

Processing the Audio

Chapter 7 explored ways to use the microphone and your voice so you have more vocal presence. Here are some technical tricks that will add to your or your interviewee's presence.

Editing packages offer a range of effects, most of which you'll never need to use when making learning content, although they are fun to play around with. After all, how will a "digital delay" effect make your voice clearer and easier to understand? And how will changing the pitch of someone's voice improve your interview? Despite the fun you may have in experimenting with them, many of the effects are pretty much useless for the serious podcaster. However, there are two that you should use to make your vocals sound superb: the graphic equalizer and the compressor.

Graphic Equalizer

The graphic equalizer enables you to make the voice crisper, clearer, and have more presence, even as many people experience a degradation in hearing quality. As we grow older, our ears become less efficient at hearing the bass and treble frequencies. So when you listen to your favorite symphony, sounds from instruments like the triangle might not be as clear. And you won't hear sounds like the hi-hat in a rock song as strongly as you did 10 years ago. However, the human ear does not tend to have any problem with middle frequencies.

When you listen to a voice-over, your ear will hear the middle frequencies clearly but miss some of the resonant bass that adds warmth and authority and the treble that gives it presence. This can make the voice feel a little lifeless. To compensate for this and ensure that the listener enjoys the full range of their voice or their interviewee's voice, audio professionals adjust the levels of certain frequencies using a graphic equalizer. Think of it as a little like the bass, middle, and treble controls on a stereo system or car radio, only more precise.

Professionals call this process "adjusting the EQ" (EQ stands for equalization). To make a voice-over sound clearer and stand out over a music bed, you can boost the higher and lower frequencies while lowering the middle frequencies. This may sound very academic, but when you listen to the difference, you'll really hear the power of adjusting the EQ (Figure 8-3).

Figure 8-3. Adjusting the EQ

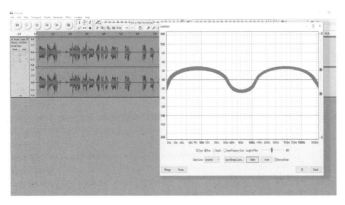

The graphic equalizer function allows you to boost different audio frequencies to make the audio easier to hear. In this example, the bass and treble frequencies are boosted, while the midrange frequencies are reduced.

Audio editing software programs provide a graphic equalizer in the effects menu, and it's valuable to experiment with it so you can hear the difference between an adjusted voice and a nonadjusted voice. As you get used to playing around with EQ, you'll recognize that certain frequency ranges offer different qualities.

To boost the warmth and presence of someone's voice, adjust the settings in the graphic equalizer so they look somewhat like a wave. You can do this by adjusting the frequencies so they are given a little boost below 250 hertz and then dip at about 250 hertz, before coming back at around 2 kilohertz and then increasing between 2 kilohertz and 4 kilohertz, as you can see in the diagram. Use these ranges as a start and experiment with them. The key to adjusting the EQ is not to memorize all the different ranges, but to listen to the voice and adjust the frequencies until it sounds warmer, clearer, and more present.

EQ is a hard concept to make sense of when written. The best way to really understand it is to play with it. So experiment with some spoken word recordings and listen to how your adjustments improve vocal quality. With practice it will become easy.

Adjusting the equalization on spoken word content will make the voice clearer and easier to pick up when combined with music and sound effects.

Compressor

Have you noticed that a lot of radio announcers have warm, full-sounding voices? Wouldn't it be nice if your e-learning or podcast voice-overs had this richness? Beyond processing their voices through the graphic equalizer, audio professionals also use an audio compressor, which thickens the voice and balances all the audio levels so the person speaking is easier to hear.

It's easy to get confused about compression because IT professionals also use the term to refer to the process of reducing file sizes, for example, when uploading content to the web. However, in this context, it refers to compressing the audio signal.

The compressor helps manage loud and soft volume levels and helps moderate them when they fluctuate. Volume often varies when we and others speak. For example, one person in your recording may speak loudly, while another person speaks softly. Some people start a sentence boisterously but trail off toward the end. All these factors make it difficult to ensure continuity in your podcast. Compression moderates the differences.

In technical terms, the compressor adjusts the volume of any sound in your recording above a certain volume level. Audio engineers call this level the threshold, similar to a thermostat on a heater. For example, if you set the threshold at -12 decibels, the compressor will kick in when any sound in your recording is louder than that threshold. So when a sound goes higher than -12 decibels, the compressor will reduce its level.

You set the ratio to determine how much the volume is adjusted per decibel when it goes above the threshold. It's best to aim for a ratio between 2:1 and 4:1. Anything higher than that will sound unnatural and become even less natural as it heads up to 10:1.

The best way to fully understand compression is to play around with it. As with EQ, any written explanation will sound dry and academic. But fire up your audio editing software, record some audio, and play around with the compressor effect. You will hear how good your voice sounds once it has been compressed, and it will be easier for the learner to hear because any highs and lows will be evened out.

Noise Removal Effect

If you've ever recorded audio or video in a room with a noisy air conditioner, you know how distracting it can be. Most audio editing software programs have an effect called noise removal that can help cure your podcasts of such background noise. Unfortunately, the only time I have ever seen noise removal work well is on *CSI: Miami,* when Horatio Caine has one of his investigators remove the background noise from a nightclub scene. Like a lot of what you see on television, it's fake. Noise removal works by sampling an element of your background, such as the loud air conditioner, which sounds like *sh.* It then goes through the whole recording and removes frequencies associated with this sample. It removes not just the air conditioner noise, but the *sh* sound from words like *should* and *shall.* It's worth playing around with this function just to satisfy your curiosity. As you do, you'll notice the whole recording just sounds odd and unnatural with this function. You can adjust the level of removal if you want to be subtle, but then what's the point? Only in TV shows does noise removal work. Ultimately, the only way to get rid of noise in the background is to find a quiet location to record in.

Multitracking

Once you've edited your spoken word content, it's time to add music, sound effects, and other segments such as panel discussions and monologues. To accomplish this, you use multitracking, the process of stacking multiple tracks and playing them at the same time (Figure 8-4). The process is similar to layers in Photoshop. Let's say the first track is your introductory monologue. Multitracking allows you to add a music track so they both play at the same time. This is one of the most exciting aspects of audio editing, but it takes practice to learn efficiently.

Figure 8.4 Multitrack

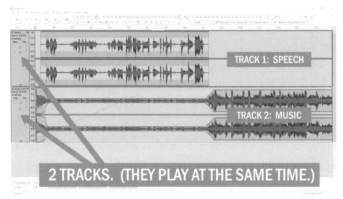

Multitracking is the process of stacking several tracks on top of one another so they all play at the same time. They are later mixed into one final track.

But there's more to multitracking than just layering tracks on top of one another. You need to adjust the volume of each track. If you play your introduction and music tracks together, the music would probably be so loud it would drown out your voice. And you will need to use the timeshifting tool to position audio elements on different tracks at different spaces along the timeline.

Audio Staircase Method

When you multitrack your audio segments, order the sequence of tracks so the track at the top of the screen is the first track to play, the one below is second, the one below that is third, and so forth. This will look like a staircase of audio tracks. Managing multiple tracks can be confusing, and this will reduce some of that. You can move tracks up and down by holding your mouse over the left control bar of each track.

Adjusting the Volume

As you mix different audio tracks together, you will need to adjust the volume level of each track. One track may be a presenter introducing the podcast. Another may be some background music. You will need to adjust the volume of the music so it does not drown out the presenter's voice.

To adjust the volume of each track, we need to go into envelope mode and use the envelope tool. You find this at the top of Audacity in the cluster of buttons that also has the selector mode button.

When you are in envelope mode, you'll see thick blue lines imposed on the outer extremities of each track. These represent the volume of your music. Along these lines you'll create marker points that indicate current and then adjusted volume. To do this, take the envelope tool and position it so the line is in the middle of the tool. Then create one mark; that's the start point. Next, create another mark and drag it down. You will see the visual representation of where the volume goes down. To bring the volume up again, you will create a marker at the point you want the volume to rise and then a second one to increase it.

Positioning Audio Elements Along the Timeline

Your podcast is going to be made up of more than just one audio element. You might have one or two interviews and some doorstop soundbites. So how do you combine them all? You can't have them all playing at the same time.

This is when you will position each element along the timeline at the point you wish them to be heard. In Audacity, this is done using the timeshift tool.

When you position your cursor on the track you want to shift, hold down the left button on the mouse and move the track from left to right. You'll see you can position it anywhere on the timeline.

Now you can create the order of each individual item in sequence.

Exporting

When you have finished building your podcast in the editing program, you will need to export it as a final media file that people can use. Most likely you'll export it as an MP3. If you intend to use the file in other podcasts or software programs, you might select WAV; the file size will be larger, but the quality will be better. Under the file menu of your audio editing program, select the export function. It will bring up a window for you to select the format and where you want to save the file. When you save the file, it will also give you the option to enter metadata.

Work Flow

As discussed in chapter 3, it's critical to develop a regular work flow to make the routine tasks habitual, freeing your mind to truly engage with the creative side of content creation. Here are some suggestions for how to sequence your editing tasks:

1. Set up your folder structure, if you haven't already done so, and save all the audio files into their respective subfolders. As you do, rename them according to your naming convention.

2. Import your audio elements into your editing software and assemble them in sequential order.

3. Position each audio element with the track along the timeline following the audio staircase method.

4. Process your audio. If you choose to add EQ and compression to the tracks, do it to every track before you start editing. That way the same settings are applied to all.

5. Perform your edits. If you are editing spoken word content and it features music in the background, or vice versa, you can click on the solo button, located on the control bar at the left of each track, so it turns off every other track and you only hear the one you are working on. Don't forget to turn the solo button off when you move to the next edit.

6. Adjust the volume. Use the envelope tool to adjust the volume of music and sound effects used behind spoken word content.

7. When you are finished, export the complete project as a final copy either as a WAV or MP3 file.

8. Get into the habit of saving regularly.

This is a good general sequence to follow, but editing is a creative process and, by its nature, an iterative experience. You will find yourself going in and out of the different editing modes to finesse aspects of your podcast. And you may import extra audio after having done most of your edits because you come up with a way to lift the overall package. This is fine. It's just important to not approach these tasks ad hoc because otherwise you may forget a step here or there, thus slowing down your audio development.

Summary

Many people who work in radio will tell you they never want to work in television because they love all that the audio modality offers to communicate rich and engaging content. And many TV pros who started in radio will look wistful when they talk about their broadcasts without pictures. Audio is special. You'll no doubt discover its magic as you work with it.

However, you of course are not creating podcasts and other audio content for your own consumption. You're doing it for the learner. This modality offers exciting ways to create learning that draws on the learner's experiences and knowledge, using the spoken word, music, and sound effects. Audio will continue to grow in popularity as more media companies produce high-quality podcasts and more people subscribe to them so they can listen during their commute or lounging around the house.

Video and Learning

In This Chapter
- What are the dynamics of video as a learning modality?
- What does the video production process look like?
- How can you improve on talking head and screen capture videos?

Video in learning is nothing new. Forty years ago, learning professionals threaded filmstrips into movie projectors, dimmed the lights, and beamed flickering educational content on the wall. They'd rent these films from libraries that supplied professionally produced educational content. Twenty years later, filmstrips were gone and educators rented VHS cassettes. They rolled heavy stands into the classroom that had TV sets and clunky old video machines mounted on them. Back in those days, those films and VHS cassettes were precious. Usually, the trainer had a single filmstrip or VHS cassette. And she kept it under lock and key because she couldn't afford to lose it—she wouldn't share it with learners to watch at home or with her colleagues for that matter, who might forget to return it.

Now, video tends to be a central file stored in the cloud that anyone can access at any time, using virtually any device. It's no longer a matter of ordering an educational video and waiting a week for it to be delivered. It's simply a matter of typing YouTube or Vimeo into a web browser.

If this is not enough, the learning professional herself now has all the tools she needs to create her own video content. And she can do it cheaply with relative ease. She's not confined to a library catalogue that offers broad and generic content. She can tailor-make video that's specific for her curriculum, her style of teaching, and the needs of her learners.

Video as a tool for learning, marketing, information, and entertainment is in a huge growth phase. Research shows that half of all mobile traffic is video, and that's only set to grow. Ericsson predicts that video will make up 70 percent of mobile traffic by 2012 (Dreier 2016). Everyone, it seems, is getting in on the video act.

This makes sense given that many people, including learning professionals, carry a video camera around in their pocket or purse; that is, a smartphone or tablet with a camera embedded in it. And they can edit their content on the fly, turning it around in no time.

However, not all video is created equal. Instructional video really only has value if someone watches it, understands it, and then applies the information. The key to attracting viewers is to create content that is engaging, which means taking advantage of everything this modality has to offer. Making it easy to understand is about being clear about your objective and making it as simple as possible.

This chapter will explore video as a modality for learning and touch on what learning professionals can do to ensure their content is engaging and leads to learning that's easy to remember and apply.

Video Forms

Learning professionals can create many forms of video, but most will use one of four forms:

- **Sequence videos** are the kind of immersive videos you watch on television, such as news stories, dramas, and documentaries. Multiple shots are edited together to convey a message in a seamless package. They draw on video techniques that have evolved since the days of the silent picture. Sequence videos, which represent the gold standard of video, rely on the pictures to carry the bulk of the story. They make the most of what video as a modality has to offer.

- **Talking head videos** feature a person talking to the camera as if talking directly to the viewer. Rather than rely on a sequence of pictures to convey the message, talking head videos rely on the speaker's words. Some people call them lecture videos. Talking head videos are common because they are quick, easy, and cheap to produce. However, they are not always effective for learning because viewers lose interest quickly and their minds start wandering for reasons we'll discuss shortly.

- **Screen capture videos** are recordings of what happens on a computer screen. They are usually used to teach computer tasks and are common in IT training. Generally, they are produced with screen capture software like Camtasia, although in theory you could produce them by simply aiming a camera at the screen, albeit with poor quality. Instructional screen capture videos generally feature a voice-over to explain what's happening on the screen.

- **Animated videos** create the illusion of motion using drawings, puppets, or models. Early animated videos, which have a precious space in American entertainment culture, were called cartoons and drawn by hand, such as Mickey Mouse and Bugs Bunny. Each frame was painstakingly crafted by an artist. Another type of animated video includes stop-motion animation, in which objects are slowly manipulated and photographed one frame at a time. In the learning ecosystem, most animated video is produced using software such as Adobe After Effects and Flash. Although these programs require a high degree of skill, software designed for novices include GoAnimate, PowToon, Toon Boom, and iClone. Animated videos are outside the scope of this book; however, many of the visual principles we discuss are still applicable.

Many learning professionals create talking head and screen capture videos because they are quick and affordable to produce. To make these forms of video more dynamic, it's important to understand the storytelling dynamics of sequence videos because they exploit all the many storytelling opportunities that video has to offer as a modality. This chapter will thus first explore video through the lens of sequence videos, then discuss talking head and screen capture videos at the end, to consider how to make them more engaging.

United Airlines: Video Is Good When You Need to Show Something

United Airlines uses video to train technicians on some of its maintenance tasks. Paula Essmeier, the maintenance training assistant manager of United's computer-based training group in Houston, believes video is ideal for learning hands-on skills. "People can read a manual all day long," she says. "But if you show them something, it is eye-opening." For practical tasks like repairing a seat in the first-class cabin of an aircraft or installing equipment, seeing how the work is done can transfer knowledge faster than having to read text and blueprints to piece elements and sequences together in your mind.

Video saves money, too: "We can't afford to send every mechanic out to an airplane." Instead of tying up important equipment so mechanics can observe maintenance tasks before practicing them, video can get people better prepared for the practical time they do spend on an aircraft.

Essmeier also points to the emotional power of video, which she used to create an inspirational piece about the United Airlines and Continental Airlines merger. By drawing on visual icons from aviation history associated with the two companies' past and incorporating music, she was able to weave an emotional narrative to help staff understand the organization's future. It was an uplifting alternative to delivering change information as a series of slides.

Her comments echo a central theme in this book: Video is good for learning content that requires you to show something. And it can deeply touch your learner.

Dynamics of Video as a Learning Modality

The most important thing to remember when creating learning videos is that this modality is all about pictures—that is, the footage used. Viewers remember what they see in your video more than what they hear. Therefore, to be an effective videographer, you need to adopt a pictures-first mindset. This means thinking about what you'll show learners more than what you'll tell them.

TV professionals talk and think in pictures rather than in words. When they plan their video, they think about what viewers will see on the screen more than what viewers will hear in a voice-over or set of dialogue. Pictures are a language of their own, complete with their own conventions for communicating, known as visual grammar, which has evolved since the earliest days of the silent movie. The process and dynamics of communicating with pictures is very different from using words and can be difficult for many, because we were trained from an early age to communicate with the written and spoken word. If you're new to video, you might find that the biggest challenge is simply to let go of the words.

The role pictures play in video can be seen in some of the highly produced commercials you see on network television. Google the popular TV ads broadcast during the Super Bowl and you'll see that the pictures carry the bulk of the message. Some ads have hardly any words.

Pictures have the power in video and carry most of the message. Alfred Hitchcock was one of the early people to teach this, saying that the "purist form of cinema is the silent picture." Cinematographers who made silent films had to rely entirely on the pictures to "do the talking." As a result, they exploited every element in each shot to convey their message, manipulating the lighting, shadows, and movement in tandem with the actors' posture and facial expressions. Even the location of props on screen and the clothes people wore was deliberate.

Words Are Shots; Sentences Are Sequences

So what does it mean to communicate in pictures rather than in words? When you were in elementary school, you were taught to communicate by choosing words and stringing them together to form a sentence. In one sense, this is what you do with video, except you use shots rather than words and sequences instead of sentences. (The shot refers to the action you film between pressing "start record" and "finish record" on your video camera.) Just as you search for the most powerful set of words to get your meaning across, you'll aim to create the best series of shots to convey the message.

Consider this sequence of shots. First, we might show a wide shot of a university campus, then cut to a close-up of a sign that has the university's name. Then we cut to an interior shot of a light-filled room with some test tubes and microscopes positioned on a bench. A woman wearing a lab coat walks in and sits at her desk. Each one of these shots tells a story. One tells us we're in a laboratory, another that the laboratory is part of a university. Another shot tells us the person is a scientist because she is wearing a lab coat and sits down at a desk near a microscope.

Every shot tells a story. Videographers take care to ensure that every element in their shots is deliberate and works for them. Failure to do so could result in having objects in the shot that send off the wrong message. One example of an element you might use to communicate part of your message is clothing. We know this woman is a scientist because she's wearing a lab coat. If the woman in the shot was a doctor, we might ask her to wear a stethoscope around her neck. If she was the manager of the lab, we might have her wear a suit. If a student, we might ask her to wear jeans and a sweatshirt.

Video Is a Series of Message Layers

As much as video is about pictures, it also uses other tools to get your message across. These can be understood as a series of message layers that build on the foundation laid by pictures:

- Pictures carry most of the message.
- Graphics, including text and animated graphics, add clarity and specificity.
- Spoken word adds emotion and specificity.
- Music adds mood, emotion, and atmosphere.
- Sound effects add power to the pictures and draw attention.

Each layer has its own grammar for conveying your message. And except for the picture layer—the foundational layer—all others are created equal. So it's best to plan your pictures first, then add other message layers to fill in parts of the story that are not immediately clear in the pictures.

For example, to convey that Paulo is late for work, you might choose the following pictures:

1. extreme wide shot of a Jeep Cherokee stuck in traffic, from the side of the road
2. close-up of the Jeep's dashboard showing the clock at 6:45 a.m.
3. mid shot of Paulo's face, sweating and looking worried
4. bird's-eye view (from the sky) of the congested highway, which zooms in on the Jeep
5. close-up of the clock on Jeep's dashboard clock as the digits change to 7:15 a.m.
6. mid shot from the side of Paulo hitting the steering wheel in frustration.

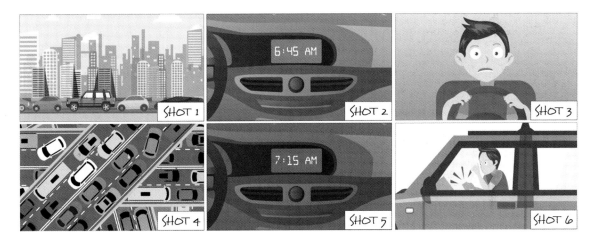

This sequence of pictures conveys a considerable amount of information, but there are still gaps in the story. For example, why is the traffic so bad? And why is Paulo stressed?

You could answer the first question by superimposing the audio of a traffic report from the radio over the picture at the precise moment the radio announcer says, "Tractor trailer accident . . . I-95 . . . three-mile traffic buildup . . ." And you could answer the second question with a kind of soliloquy where Paulo thinks out loud, with a voice-over asking, "How am I going to make the big meeting?" To create the effect that he is thinking this in his head, you could add some reverb to his voice. To add anxiety you could find some music that sounds busy and chaotic.

You'll notice that none of these message layers duplicate each other. The sound effect of the radio traffic report is the only layer conveying why traffic is delayed. The music layer is the only layer carrying the stress. The spoken word layer, which is in fact his internal voice, tells the viewer it's an important meeting.

As a learning professional playing the role of videographer, your job is to use pictures to teach. Then you draw on the additional message layers to fill in what the pictures are unable to teach. Approaching video as a series of message layers helps to prioritize the production.

The Rapid Media Technique and Video

Video production is more time intensive than audio and requires considerably more planning. So exactly how long does it take to produce video? This is difficult to answer concretely because every project is different. A 30-second sequence in a cinematic motion picture might take a cumulative week to shoot and produce, whereas 45 seconds of local news might be turned around in just a few hours.

However, putting a caveat on the fact that this can change from project to project, a ballpark figure for a polished sequence video similar to a TV news report would be about five hours of production time for each minute of final video. It's helpful to communicate this to clients and bosses who invariably think video production can happen at the snap of the fingers. Breaking it down, plan to spend roughly 40 percent of the time planning, 20 percent shooting the footage, and 40 percent editing it.

Planning the Video

Much like with audio production, planning is the most important stage of video production. It's now you write the learning objective and ask the question, "Is video the best modality for this learning topic?" Then you break the topic into chunks and form a narrative structure. This structure is the basis for your storyboard, which you will refer to when writing the script. When the script is finished, you'll create a shot plan and prepare logistics such as applying for permission to film, if shooting in public areas; clearing copyright; and making sure everyone involved knows what they're responsible for and where to turn up for the shoot.

Creating the Video

The create stage is when you actually start filming. It's the part of the process many people enjoy most. Ironically, it's the production stage that takes the least amount of time. But you can make mistakes, such as underexposed shots, poor white balance, and rolling the camera too late. Some mistakes can be fixed or improved in the edit, but correction adds lots of time. Other mistakes will require you to go back and shoot again. So the aim for this stage is not just capturing the footage, but capturing it correctly the first time, which takes skill and planning.

Editing the Video

The edit stage is when you assemble the video, graphics, and audio files into one final package. It starts with positioning the media assets on the timeline or into the storyboard window and then progresses with you manipulating them so they run together seamlessly.

Universal Content Principles for Video

In chapter 2, we discussed universal principles that apply to good content, whether it's audio, video, text, or graphics. We also looked at content mindsets to make your learning content more engaging. Let's look at how they relate specifically to video.

- **The Short Principle: Viewers have very short concentration spans**. In fact, YouTube published figures showing that when people watch online video at their desktop, they allow about two minutes (Follett 2015). People watching on a smartphone allow two to three minutes. So is there a perfect length for video? Probably not. A creative videographer can keep viewers engaged for longer periods of time. The point is to keep your instructional videos as short as you can. If there are any pictures that do not constructively add to the narrative, cut them out. If you like the music you have chosen but it doesn't add mood, energy, or atmosphere relevant to the learning objective, consider removing or replacing it. The two- to three-minute rule is probably a good one to follow, except when the topic needs more time to be explained.

- **The Simple Principle: Keep your shots uncluttered, removing props, backgrounds, or other visual elements that force your viewer's brain to do more interpretive work than necessary.** If you're shooting in someone's office and there's a snow globe from her recent vacation, ask yourself, "Does this help the message or distract from it?" It is most likely irrelevant, so remove it. Likewise, don't over-produce the video with special effects and fancy transitions. Always ask, "How does this help my viewer learn to do *X*?"

- **The Familiarity Principle: When you write your script, make sure you use words your viewer will understand, avoiding verbosity and technical jargon.** Likewise make sure your shots show body language and facial expressions your viewer is familiar with. Use locations your viewer is familiar with, too. This has implications across cultures.

- **The Emotion Principle: Video is terrific for getting people emotionally involved in the content.** Show people and their eyes. Use music to affect the mood and atmosphere. Use teasers to make viewers believe they'll miss out on something important if they stop watching now. For example, the presenter in your video may say, "Let's answer that question in a moment. First, consider this." And then a little later, "We still have to answer that question and we'll get there soon."

- **The Creative Repetition Principle: Video offers loads of opportunities to repeat key messages in different ways.** Use text graphics, voice-overs, interviews, or role plays with different people, action replays, and demonstrations.
- **The Change Principle: It is standard television practice to regularly change the shot every five to 15 seconds.** But this principle extends beyond just the pictures. Surprise people by adding new music for short amounts of time, text graphics, and sound effects. And keep the voice of anyone on the video dynamic within the 4*P*s we discussed in chapter 7.

Incorporating these principles may at first feel overwhelming, so give yourself time to adopt them. It's easier to focus on applying one principle to your video practice at a time, adding others as you become more proficient. The same applies for learning the digital media mindsets. Pick one and explore it until it's a habit, then move on to the next one. Let's consider the first two digital media mindsets as they apply to video (modality and platform sensitivity) and explore two additional mindsets that will help make sure that your video content is engaging.

- **Modality sensitivity:** Use video for action. If the topic relies mostly on words to carry the message, consider a different modality. Video is about showing action and constantly changing shots, so aim to shoot more than just talking head or screen capture videos. Bring in as many pictures to carry your message as you can and exploit each message layer, such as music and sound effects, to engage your learners. We'll talk more about this in chapter 10.
- **Platform sensitivity:** Find out how most of your viewers will access the video and produce the video that works best on that platform. For example, if your learners are watching video on their smartphones, keep them short and avoid wide shots, which lose detail on small screens. Minimize camera movement (but not necessarily the action), which can appear jerky when streamed over the Internet and also increases video file sizes. Avoid distracting transitions.
- **Cognitive load sensitivity:** Don't make your learner do more work than necessary to decode your message. Review your video and ask, "What can I take out of this video without undermining the objective?" One place to start is with the "nice to have" shots and effects that don't add to the message. Do you really need that nice time-lapse shot—what does it do to help learning? How about that music playing in the background—what's it doing for your message?
- **Audience exclusivity:** It's easy to lose sight of who your core audience is and play to more than one. Keep your audience persona nearby to ensure that you don't accidentally use words, languages, icons, or other elements that won't work.

Talking Heads and Screen Captures

Earlier in this chapter we discussed different categories of video. Much of what we explored was in the context of sequence video rather than talking heads and screen captures. How can you take these principles and apply them when you're not creating sequences?

Talking Head Videos

Talking head videos tend to be one static shot that doesn't change, sometimes for 10 to 60 minutes. This is a recipe for boredom and flies in the face of the video best practice to change the shot every 10 to 15 seconds.

In addition, the message is carried in the words of the speaker, rather than in the pictures. However, people don't listen to video, they watch it. Much of what is being presented will be lost if the video is just one person talking into the camera.

So what can we do? To counteract the lack of shot changes, use your editing program to cut in and out of the shot. For example, if you shoot the video as wide shot—that is, we see the whole person in the shot—then use the cropping tool in your editing software to cut in to a mid shot every 10 to 15 seconds. A mid shot would show the speaker from the waist up. Then cut back to the wide shot 15 seconds or so later.

To overcome the challenge of spoken words being lost, use text graphics to summarize key words. You can either use the speaker's PowerPoint slides or create your own. The slides need to contain very short pieces of information, not more than 10 to 15 words. And hold the slide long enough for the viewer to read it twice. Use your editing program to drop these slides in over the speaker as he talks. Using text graphics offers the added benefit of another shot change.

Screen Capture Videos

Screen capture videos can be dry and uninteresting. What makes them less appealing is that your learner does not see the person speaking. All she sees is a piece of inanimate software that the video producer is moving a mouse around. Another challenge is that the audio is often boring and recorded on a headset mic.

So, to make your screen capture video more engaging, make it personal. When you record the screen capture, set up a camera and speak to it as you record instructions. Then cut between your head and the screen capture. This gives you shot changes and makes it more personal.

You'll recall from chapter 6 that we discussed the significant limitations of headset mics, along with the pros and cons of different microphones. If you're using a headset mic, ditch it and buy an unobtrusive lavalier mic, which you can clip onto your shirt. Plug this into your camera and use the camera audio for your voice and computer audio for mouse clicks. Finally, add music every once in a while to boost the energy.

Summary

Video is not a new tool for learning professionals; the ability for them to make polished, engaging instructional videos themselves is what's new. While the thought of making video may be intimidating, it is much easier when you approach it as a series of message layers and invest time in planning. So where do you start?

Chapter 10 will explore things you need to plan before going out and shooting your video. Good planning will save you time and money. In chapter 11, the focus is on video equipment. Knowing what to look for when choosing equipment can be overwhelming, so this chapter looks at the core essentials. Chapter 12 explores the process of shooting video and how to get pictures that look professional and draw the viewer into your story. And in chapter 13, we'll explore editing.

Planning Video Content

In This Chapter
· What are the picture message layer and supporting layers?
· How do you plan video production?
· What's the best way to handle project administration?

The secret to producing engaging video without wasting time is planning. But planning video content and production is much more complex than planning audio because you need to juggle many tasks. On one hand, you have the editorial decisions, which involve balancing multiple message layers to ensure your learning objective is met. On the other, you have the production tasks, which have many moving parts.

Instructional video starts its life much as audio does. You identify the learning objective, then ask the modality question: Is video the best modality for this topic? Assuming it is, you then break the content into chunks and form a structure, possibly using the ROPS model.

It's after this initial work has been done that the production tasks specific to video need to be addressed. These include turning your structure into a visual sequence, using a storyboard, and adding supporting message layers to fill in the gaps. Once this is done, it's down to production logistics that ensure filming and editing are done efficiently and minimize the risk of disruption when filming.

In this chapter, we will start by exploring the editorial dimensions of planning video content, which revolve around the pictures. Then we'll look at issues for production planning and project administration.

Objective and Structure

Chapter 5 discussed what a learning objective is and why having one is so important for digital content production. It looked at breaking the learning objective into chunks and using the ROPS model as a template to plan the sequence. However, ROPS is not the only way to structure your learning. Traditional story structures work really well too. For example, if you need to teach the value of mentoring programs, you could bring your video to life by showing the story of a new recruit who is mentored by a senior manager and works through some professional trials with the manager's support and guidance, going on to build a successful career. This beats a sterile presentation on why mentoring is good and how it works because stories organize the information in a way that's easy to remember; when we see someone else, we're drawn to it.

Storytelling has flourished as an art in every culture since ancient times. Aristotle and Plato were probably the earliest philosophers to talk about plot and characterization. As an overview of four different digital modalities, this book does not have the space to explore storytelling and do it justice. As such, the ROPS template is the vehicle we use to consider how to structure digital learning. However, you can explore the details of storytelling in some excellent books. Robert McKee wrote the classic *Story* for cinema, which has influenced numerous Hollywood films and suggests there are 21 major plots. Christopher Booker wrote *The Seven Basic Plots*, which at 700 pages provides incredible depth. More recently, Lisa Cron wrote *Wired for Story*, which draws on cognitive neuroscience.

The Picture Message Layer

Chapter 9 broke down the value of drawing the storyboard before you write the script. Doing it in this order surprises some people, especially those who have traditionally penned their script first and then gone hunting for pictures. But learners will remember the pictures in your video more than the words. So it makes sense to start with pictures and invest most of your time deliberating on the pictures rather than the words.

The video storyboard sets out each individual shot that you will use to convey the story. The bigger the production, the more detail it will provide. Once complete, you will refer to it to select the supporting message layers, such as the spoken word, music, and sound effects.

The storyboard is not used only by the producer and writer. The camera operator will also use it on location to be sure he is getting pictures the way the writer intends, and the editor will work from it to ensure she cuts the pictures together in a way that is faithful to the story.

Before you draw a storyboard, it is helpful to understand some of the dynamics about how to use pictures to tell stories. When videographers plan their pictures they consider how different shot sizes, camera angles, and camera movements can help make their message clearer.

Shot Sizes

Shot sizes describe how close the camera (and as a result the learner) is to the person or object in your video. They balance the amount of context and intimacy in your shot. All in all, there are about nine shot sizes and each one falls into one of the following three categories (Table 10-1):

- wide shot, also known as long shot
- mid shot
- close-up.

Table 10-1. Examples of Shot Sizes

	**Wide Shot** Wide shots (WS), like the image on the left, provide the viewer with context and are often used to establish a scene. The standard WS captures a person from head to toe. There's also an extreme wide shot (XWS), which is all about the environment. You would hardly notice people in this kind of shot.
	**Mid Shot** The mid shot (MS) balances both context and intimacy. It shows the person, body language, and some broad facial expressions while also providing some contextual reference. This is the most natural shot because it replicates the general distance people stand from each other. A medium close-up (MCU) would frame the person from just above the elbows and is ideal for subject matter expert interviews.
	**Close-Up** The close-up (CU) is the most intimate shot because it's all about the person and the environment is no longer in shot. CUs are unnatural because they position the viewer much closer than the viewer would ordinarily stand to someone else. Going closer than the CU to show just the eyes or mouth is known as an extreme close-up (XCU). However, this is even more unnatural and might be off-putting to your viewer.

Camera Angles

The camera angle determines who has power between the object or person in shot and the viewer. When the camera looks up at an object or person, that object or person will seem big and more powerful. This is known as a low-angle shot because we look up at the person from a low angle. If the camera looks down at the person, the viewer has the power and the person in shot looks more vulnerable. This is known as a high-angle shot. If the camera angle looks directly across at the person, the viewer will feel on equal footing, which is known as an eye-level shot.

Camera angles save us adding information about status to other message layers. For example, if you shoot a leadership video, you can use a low-angle shot to imply someone is a leader and avoid the need to include a caption that says "boss."

The illustrations in Table 10-2 are slightly exaggerated for effect. However, when using them in your video, keep them subtle so they won't distract the learner from the content.

More Ideas to Spruce Up Talking Head Videos

People often ask me how they can make their talking head videos more interesting. You may face a similar challenge. The simple answer is you can't. However, the good news is you can at least make them less boring. There will be times when you have no choice but to shoot a lecture as a simple talking head. The challenge for talking head videos is how to keep eyeballs from wandering. One approach is to use two cameras. Have one camera capture a wide shot and another a mid shot from a different position. You can cut between these two shots regularly. If you only have one camera, use editing software to cut in and out using its crop feature. If the speaker uses PowerPoint, get a copy, export the slides as JPGs, and drop them into the edited version. This way you can cut between a wide shot, a mid shot, and the PowerPoint slides. Don't use video footage of the slides that was filmed during the presentation because it will look amateurish. If there are no slides, create some yourself. If possible, shoot some footage of the audience and cut in and out of that as well, while the speaker is talking. If your lecture is 60 minutes, package it into six 10-minute lectures, providing a quick summary of what has been learned so far at the beginning of module.

Table 10-2. Examples of Camera Angles

	**Low-Angle Shot** Low-angle shots give power to the person in shot. Good for portraying leaders, teachers, authority figures, and other people you want the viewer to look up to.
	**Eye-Level Shot** Eye-level shots establish the person in the shot as the same status as the viewer. Good for interviews and talking head shots.
	**High-Angle Shot** High-angle shots give power to the viewer. These are good for portraying victims or direct reports and creating a sense of control for the viewer.

Camera Movement

Camera movements can make your shots more interesting and add narrative value. For example, if there's no action in your shot, such as a talking head video, a slow zoom may create the effect of change and keep the viewer engaged. Camera movements can tell part of the story too. To create the effect that you are traveling somewhere, you might use a dolly shot. Camera moves do not play smoothly over the Internet and if you use too many, they can be distracting.

Table 10-3 describes the common terms for camera movement.

Table 10-3. Terms for Camera Movement

	**Pan Left or Right** This is where the camera pivots from left to right. Pan is shortened from the word panorama.
	**Zoom In or Out** This is where you change the focal length of the lens while the video is rolling, creating the effect of moving closer to or farther from the person or object in shot.
	**Tilt Up or Down** This is where the camera pivots up and down. This can be good for showing power.
	**Crab Left or Right** This is where the camera literally moves from left to right or right to left. This move is also known as track left or right, truck left or right, or dolly left or right.
	**Dolly In or Out** This is where the camera physically moves closer (in) to the subject or object or away (out) from the subject or object. The terms *truck in* and *truck out* or *track in* and *track out* are also used.

Zoom In Versus Dollying In

Close-up achieved by dollying in   Close-up achieved by zooming in

The difference between zooming in, which involves changing the focal length of your lens, and dollying in, which involves physically moving the camera closer, can be confusing. Are they the same? Not quite. When you zoom in, you are creating an optical illusion of closeness and the outer extremities of your frame will be exactly the same when you are zoomed in or out. When you dolly in, the outer extremities of the frame will change as the lens gets closer.

Planning Your Shots and the Storyboard

When you draw your storyboard, you will be thinking of each shot in terms of its shot size, the camera angle, and any camera movement. You will also be thinking about what action takes place in the shot. Drawing a storyboard can be intimidating if you don't draw well. But it's a valuable process because it trains the brain to think in pictures.

The storyboard process is especially important if you've spent most of your life writing content because your natural bias will be to use words to communicate. In video, you need to use pictures. Drawing each shot will force you to think about that picture, how it works with other pictures, and the movement the viewer will see. If you're worried about your artistic skills, don't fret. Storyboards are not art and will work just as effectively with stick figures.

Working with a storyboard saves you time. It helps you be more directed on location, saving you from guessing what shots you think may be important. Without a storyboard, you will find yourself shooting much more footage than you would ever use.

Many learning professionals use storyboards in e-learning development. However, these are different from video storyboards, which require each frame to be drawn out with a description of shot size, camera angle, and camera movement.

Putting Pictures in Order

Think carefully about the order in which your shots will appear. This affects the ease with which your viewer will be able to follow your message. Start by considering the order that creates a logical flow. Then think about shot changes to keep the viewer's attention.

As a general rule, you should start with a wide shot to establish the context. This is a common technique used across television. If you have ever watched an episode of the TV series *Seinfeld,* you'll see that before any scene in the coffee shop, they show an external wide shot of the coffee shop to establish where the scene takes place.

Some people plan their action sequences using shot formulas. The most common are the three-shot and five-shot formulas. Many news camera operators follow the three-shot formula. When they are on scene, they shoot three takes of the same action from three different positions. Usually the positions will be:

- wide shot
- close-up
- mid shot.

If you are shooting a sequence where a woman walks into a room and sits at her desk, you might shoot a wide shot of her entering the room, walking to her desk, and sitting down. You'll then repeat the action and film a close-up of her face walking toward the camera, and then a mid shot from the side as she sits at her desk. When you get to the edit, you will cut these three shots together so it's not simply a boring wide shot.

The five-shot formula follows the same principles, only it includes two additional shots. This technique, often used in digital documentaries, creates more visual interest but takes longer to shoot. The shots are:

- wide shot
- extreme close-up
- close-up
- mid shot
- creative shot.

The creative shot should be unexpected or unconventional to attract the viewer's eye. If the sequence is in an office, the creative shot may show the action taking place through the window. Once again, the editor will cut these five shots together to create a sequence that is interesting.

Supporting Message Layers

The principle of starting with your pictures is based on the assumption that people remember what they see more than what they hear. So it's important to pack as much of the message into the picture as you can. That means planning the backdrop to convey part of the message, adding props, wearing appropriate clothes, and directing body language and movement.

But no matter how good you are at exploiting every opportunity a picture offers, there will be some messages you just need extra help with. And that's where the supporting layers come in. Their role is to fill in the narrative gaps the picture can't fill. Let's quickly look at supporting message layers and then the mechanics of the script, which captures all the information needed to shoot your video.

Pitney Bowes: A Deliberate Approach to Video

Technology company Pitney Bowes has its own in-house production process for creating learning video. Headquartered in Connecticut, the company manufactures office equipment such as franking machines and mail sorters. Jesse Johns runs its Global Service Center of Expertise in Georgia and takes a balanced view of video. "Video is not the solution but rather part of the solution," he says. "The biggest temptation in creating videos is creating video for the sake of creating video." He warns against seeing it merely as a new toy: "There is a time and place for video."

Pitney Bowes produces video that is used in many different areas. In the classroom, it is used to demonstrate difficult tasks such as removing and replacing parts in expensive machinery, which is costly to take offline for demonstrations. During lab exercises, learners access video to help them self-pace their learning. The company compiles the clips in video libraries so people can easily access the content outside the class. And it embeds videos within e-learning programs.

What advice does Johns offer to learning executives introducing video into their delivery strategy? "Be aware that it is a learning curve." He adds that resources and time are big obstacles, so having a good work flow is the key to producing video when appropriate for the learning need.

The Spoken Word

Video writing conventions are very similar to those discussed in chapter 5 about audio writing. You will make your content quicker and easier to understand if you adopt a conversational tone; use short, concrete words; and construct short sentences. But there's an added dimension to video writing that doesn't apply to audio, generally referred to as "writing to picture." Don't repeat the picture in your script; rather, add what's not clear.

Let's say you are shooting an onboarding video and plan a sequence where a young woman walks into the main lobby of your organization. Adding the voice-over, "This woman is walking into the lobby," is redundant because we can already see that. However, it's not obvious who she is or why she is in the lobby. So rather than repeat what's obvious, your voice-over should be something like, "Meghan's first day."

Music

Music is good for influencing mood, creating atmosphere, and adding energy. It can also provide narrative detail. For example, if you want to portray someone as busily running around, you could use Rimsky-Korsakov's well-known orchestral piece, "The Flight of the Bumblebee," behind a sequence of fast-motion videos—perhaps a character frantically getting ready for work. As powerful as music is, resist the temptation to run the same piece of music for the entire video because it will lose its effect after a short while. And be careful about the criteria you use to select music. It's easy to choose music based on your personal preferences. But music in an instructional video is not for enjoyment or entertainment. It has a narrative purpose, so choose music in terms of what mood, atmosphere, and energy it will bring to your video.

Sound Effects

In cinema and high-end television drama, the sounds you hear are generally added on during the edit. If you hear a car door closing, it is most likely not the real door. This is because the microphones are usually positioned to pick up the characters' voices, not the sounds given off by objects. Dubbing sound effects will certainly add to your video. If you choose to, plan time to either find the sound effects from a library or record them yourself.

Graphics

Graphics are still images that support the pictures. They may be diagrams, text, or photographs that are manipulated to convey a message. Text graphics can display keywords or points you want to reinforce, helping with creative repetition in the learning video. Graphics work best when they are simple.

Script Mechanics

When you have finished the storyboard and determined what additional message layers you will use, it's time to write the script. It doesn't really matter how you lay out your script so long as anyone working with you can understand it.

A common approach to script layout is the three-column format (Figure 10-1). The first column lists the shot number, which relates to the shot plan (discussed in the next section). The second column describes what's on the screen; for example, "Wide shot of Freda Bloomsbury lifting boxes onto shelf in aisle 47." The third column contains the audio, which includes spoken word content, music, and sound effects.

Figure 10-1. Script in 3-Column Format

Workplace Safety Video
Writer: Tanya Smith
Phone: x6764
Date: 7/28/16

1	EXTERNAL: Extra-wide shot of a warehouse entrance	Short music piece. Fades as we cut to shot 3.
2	INTERNAL: Wide shot of Freda Bloomsbury lifting boxes onto a shelf in aisle 47	
3	INTERNAL: Mid shot of Freda as she places a box on the middle shelf, then turns to the camera	**Freda:** It's easy to get hurt.
4	INTERNAL: Wide shot of a forklift moving boxes into aisle 47	**Freda:** That's why we're serious about safety everywhere in the warehouse.
5	INTERNAL: Mid shot of Freda standing in front of the shelf, talking to the camera	**Freda:** Something as simple as lifting a box can do it.

Production Planning

When you've done the storyboard and script, it's time to plan the production. Here are some of the important things to consider.

Shot Plan

Before you pick up your camera and head out to film your script, plan the order in which you will film each shot. The best approach is to film all scenes from one location at the same time, even if the video does not run in that order. For example, if you have a five-minute video and three scenes are in the lobby of a building, four scenes in the parking lot, and four in a restaurant, you should shoot all the lobby shots together, all the parking lot scenes together, and all the restaurant shots together. The only times you will change this is if you need to shoot them at different times of day, such as one scene in the early morning and the others at dusk.

Your shot plan can follow any format that works for you and your team. But you might want to consider including the following information (Figure 10-2):

- location
- shot number—this is from the first column of the script
- time scheduled for filming
- actors required and how they should be dressed
- crew required
- additional notes.

Figure 10-2. Sample Shot Plan

Location	Shots	Time for Filming	Actors Required	Dress & Props	Crew Required	Additional Notes
GM's office	2, 5, 7, 11	8-10 a.m.	Bob, Michelle	Business suits. Michelle needs her iPhone.	Brian, Samantha, Peter	GM needs her office back for a 10:15 a.m. meeting. Finish shots as early as possible.
Factory floor outside the door to lunchroom 3	3, 9	10:30-11:05 a.m.	Regina	Working clothes. Bring clipboard.	Brian, Samantha, Peter	Regina is coming straight from a meeting and may be five minutes late.

Location	Shots	Time for Filming	Actors Required	Dress & Props	Crew Required	Additional Notes
Factory lunchroom 3	4, 6, 10	2:30-3:30 p.m.	Michelle, Brandy, Roger, Pike	Workers clothes. Make sure each has a lunchbox with food to nibble on during the shot	Brian, Samantha, Peter	The lunchroom will be closed to staff from 2 to 4 p.m. so we can shoot undisturbed. Create a sign for the door to redirect staff to lunchrooms 1 and 2.
Factory gate at west Entrance	1, 8, 12	4:30-5:30 p.m.	Bob	Business suit. Need the Lexus because Bob drives out of the gate in scene 12.	Brian, Samantha, Pedro, and Security Officer to manage pedestrians.	Security will tell us who is helping us for this scene at 6 p.m. the night before the shoot, once the rosters are finalized.

Location Plan

Before you film at any location, check if you need permission. You don't want to arrive with all your equipment and be asked to leave by a security officer. Many public venues require a permit from the city or town. If you are filming in a school where minors may be caught on camera, you should contact the school administration first. If you want to film in a public space within an office building where members of the public walk by, or in a factory where staff are busy at work, inform facilities management of your intentions. They can coordinate your shoot and work with security if necessary. Some organizations, such as health companies, government agencies, and hospitals, need to protect confidential information and the identities of people they care for, so they are very strict when someone turns up to film without permission.

In addition, before you start filming, go out and scout the location. Walk around and look at where you will position actors and what backdrops will help convey the message. Make sure you visit at the same time of day you plan to shoot because it will give you a sense of how it will look with the position of the sun and any other factors that might affect filming, like traffic. You don't want to plan a powerful shot and then find out that you're shooting into the sun or that students from the local high school take a shortcut through your set at 3 p.m. every day.

When you scout the location, take note of anything that might cause problems. What could go wrong and either cause you bodily harm or damage your equipment? Conducting a basic risk assessment means thinking through what risks exist and avoiding them.

Project Administration

Your production experience will go much quicker if you establish some basic administrative practices and follow them consistently. You should have a system to manage files, which chapter 13 will discuss. If you work with a team you should agree with team members on the best way to communicate and keep everyone up-to-date with progress.

Responsibility Chart

Be clear about who is responsible for the various tasks that need to be performed in your video project. The bigger your team, the more important this clarity is. If working with one or two people, you can assign responsibilities in a simple email. But for larger groups that may also involve stakeholders like subject matter experts, people from the legal department, and even branding or marketing staff, draw up a responsibility chart (Figure 10-3).

Figure 10-3. Sample Responsibility Chart

Action	Brian (Video Lead)	Samantha (Admin)	Pedro (Training Dept.)	Andre (SME)	Michelle (Legal Dept.)
Learning objective	R		T	S	I
Structure	T		T	I	I
Storyboard	T		R	S	
Script	T		I	S	S
Location and shot plan	T, S	T	I	I	
Shooting the video (including lights and sound)	T	T	R	I	
Edit the video	T		R	S	S
Copyright clearance	I	R	R	I	S
Final review and project close	I	I	T	T	I

R = Provides resources to assist

S = Signs off on work when complete

I = Needs to be informed on progress of this task

T = Performs the task

Communication Plan

The bigger your team, the more communication can become a point of contention. Put together a list of who needs to know what. There's an old adage that you can never communicate too much, but that's simply an overreaction to people who fail to communicate enough. People are too busy today to be bombarded with emails that are not immediately relevant. So agree at the outset what you will send out and who will receive it.

Agreements With Stakeholders

If you are working with subject matter experts, establish a sign-off policy. As the producer, your responsibility is to produce the video and make it quick and easy for the viewer to understand. But unless you're also the SME, you're not responsible for the accuracy of its content. That belongs to the SME.

Working with SMEs can be challenging at times; they tend to be very passionate about putting in as much information as they can but might not understand how to communicate with video. So establish clear boundaries for what they have a say on and what they don't.

Another problem that often crops up when working with subject matter experts is that they ask for changes at a stage of the production process that is disruptive and time-consuming. For example, as they sit with you while you edit, they notice an object in a shot that should not be there and demand you go back and reshoot it. To avoid this, have your subject matter expert sign off on content at critical stages of production. Agree with your SME that once that stage has been signed off on, you will not go back. If the project can't go forward without re-filming something, it needs to become a new project and start in line after your other upcoming projects.

Here are some key stages to consider having your SME sign off on:

- learning objectives
- breakdown of the content and how it is structured
- storyboard
- script
- filming—have them on location with you and get them to sign off on each shot
- the accuracy of the edit—not the style.

Remember that the SME's job is to ensure accuracy, not style and form. Your job is to take the content and make it quick and easy to understand. By all means encourage their input on style, but be clear that you have the final say on how it's shot and how it looks.

Century 21: Preparation Is Key

Stephanie Singh, manager of online platform content at Century 21 Real Estate's corporate university, says preparation is key to being able to consistently deliver good-quality video. "Be as prepared as you possibly can before the shoot and take the time to write a great script," she says. It's not just editorial preparation that is key, though. "Setting up the shot on the day, checking white balance, exposure, and focus, and setting correct audio levels really pays off in postproduction. You get beautiful pictures and clear audio."

Singh's videos are generally one to two minutes long, focused on one topic only, and used in synchronous and asynchronous online learning. They include news items, testimonials, and interviews that support the learning content. Her focus on preparation goes beyond just shooting and editing the video; it includes preparing talent to appear on camera. For one big project that involved interviewing 20 people, she started months in advance: "We had a webinar for [people appearing in interviews] to help prepare them for the shoot. [We went through] what to wear, how to sit, voice levels, and things to avoid."

Singh is quick to point out that most of her team has not been formally trained in videography, but they've been getting great feedback for their work. This is great inspiration if you're just starting out.

Summary

The more you plan, the quicker and easier your shoot will be. You'll shoot the footage faster because everything is ready to go. You'll have less distractions from last-minute things that pop up, which could have been prevented with basic planning, that take your focus away from setting up the shots correctly. And, you'll have the mental space to be creative. Winging it can cost you extra time and lead to much frustration.

Proper planning is not the only thing you need to do to rapidly produce learning video; you also need to use your video equipment properly. But before we get into using video equipment, we need to consider the equipment you need. That's what we'll focus on in the next chapter. Then, in chapter 12, we'll look at how to save time by using your video equipment properly.

Your Video Toolkit

In This Chapter

- What should you look for when buying a camera?
- What camera and production accessories are essential or optional?

If you've ever spent time doing DIY work around your house, you'll know how important it is to have the right tool for the right task. For example, it's difficult to cut 45-degree angles on base-boards without a miter saw, just as it is hard to screw a Phillips-head screw with a flat-head screw-driver. Yes, you can do it, but it's not easy and takes longer.

As important as it is to have the right tools, it's also important to have good-quality tools. Buy a $1 paintbrush and some of the bristles will fall out, sticking in your paint, causing you to waste time picking them out. A few extra dollars will get you a better quality paintbrush that doesn't have bristles that fall out and saves you time. That said, you don't need to spend $20 on a paintbrush—that's overdoing it.

Your video equipment doesn't have to be ridiculously expensive, even though some may attempt to convince you otherwise. If you walk into a camera shop or search online for video equipment, the choices can be overwhelming. Does that camera cost too much? And how about the reviews? Some reviewers describe the camera as awful, while others say it's the best they've ever used. The only way to overcome this uncertainty is to know what equipment you will need and what features you won't be able to do without.

This chapter will discuss using the most affordable consumer equipment you can find that offers you the minimum features you need to make good video. You don't need to shell out $1,000 to create polished video. In fact, you can do it for considerably less.

4 Principles for Selecting Video Equipment

This chapter is based on four principles. The first is to be brand agnostic but feature conscious. It's not productive to start out looking for a Sony, Canon, or Panasonic. First look for features and then match them to a brand or model that suits your price point.

The second principle is about control. The videographer, not the camera, needs to control how the picture looks. Cameras come with all sorts of auto functions that certainly make life easier. But they can prevent you from making important decisions, such as who or what is in focus and how the shot should be exposed.

Third, simplicity is best. Today's cameras offer so many features that it's easy to find yourself spending more time trying to figure out the menu than shooting video. Many functions offered by cameras are mere bells and whistles that can make shooting for the average person more frustrating than it needs to be.

The fourth principle is that video is about the story, not your equipment. Some people are drawn to video because it offers a chance to play with a video camera. That's understandable because video cameras are a lot of fun, especially for those who are technically minded. But we shouldn't live for the camera; we need to live for the story. At the end of the day, your camera is just a tool that positions your viewer where he can see the action. It's easy to be caught up in the toys rather than the content.

So let's look at the gear that will help you shoot video. First we'll look at various types of cameras. Then we'll discuss camera accessories, production accessories, and editing software.

Different Types of Video Cameras

Cameras roughly fall into one of the following five categories (Table 11-1):

1. **Embedded cameras:** These cameras are built into devices like smartphones and tablets. Immediately available for consumers to capture video when the opportunity arises, embedded cameras have a picture quality that gets better every year. These cameras have small lenses and usually run on auto functions.

2. **Consumer cameras:** These are the cameras you have seen people recording family memories with over the years. They're light, small enough to fit in your palm, and range in cost from $100 to more than $1,000. This range covers a huge array of features and quality.

3. **DSLR cameras:** These cameras were originally single lens reflex cameras. But now many have video functionality and audio capture built into them. A benefit of DSLRs is the ability to switch out lenses, something most prosumer cameras cannot do.

4. **Prosumer cameras:** Increasingly used by television stations and news crews, they're between the consumer-level cameras and more expensive professional cameras used by network television. Prosumer cameras range between $1,800 and $4,000.

5. **Professional cameras:** These are the heavy-duty cameras used for filming network TV programs like *Dancing With the Stars,* the Super Bowl, documentaries, and dramas. They cost anywhere from $10,000 to $100,000, and that doesn't always include the cost of the lens.

Most learning professionals are unlikely to have the money for a professional camera nor the time to learn all of its functions. Prosumer cameras will be out of reach for many too. Cell phones, tablets, or consumer cameras are likely to be the first option for most, while some enthusiasts will opt for DSLRs. Because of this, let's focus on consumer cameras. However, this chapter will also explore how to get the best out of cameras embedded in cell phones and tablets.

Table 11-1. Types of Cameras

	Embedded Camera
	Consumer Camera
	DSLR Camera
	Prosumer Camera
	Professional Camera

What You Need in a Video Camera

Talk to a television professional and she'll tell you your camera needs an external microphone, manual controls, and detachable lenses.

You'll remember from chapter 6 that microphones have to be close to the sound or person you are recording. But camera mics are usually mounted on top of the camera and are too far away to capture acceptable sound. So you will need an external microphone that you can position near the audio source. You should also choose the mic that best suits your purpose: shotgun, lavalier, or interview.

Professionals want to control how their picture looks. This is why they like to have manual controls on their camera. Auto functions take this control away and cede important production decisions to the computer chip in the camera.

Having a camera that allows you to use different lenses gives the camera operator much more control over how the camera handles depth of field, lighting, and zoom. Most consumer and prosumer cameras do not have detachable lenses.

As a learning professional new to video, should you look for all these features in your consumer camera? The first two are essential, but detachable lenses add cost and are probably more complex than the average learning professional needs.

What's the Cheapest Camera I Can Get Away With?

When I was running the BBC's television training department, I asked a senior camera specialist, "What's the cheapest camera on the market I can use to get broadcast-quality video?" He turned to me and said, "You're asking the wrong question. You should be asking, 'What is the lowest level of skills you can get by with.'" Wise words. I meet a lot of people who have been sucked into buying an expensive camera and shoot video that's worse than what I see shot on cheaper consumer cameras. The bells and whistles of your camera do not make good video. It's how you use its core functions. If you want to become a phenomenal camera operator, don't spend your time researching camera models to see which one does face recognition and which one makes coffee. Instead, invest your time reading up on how to use it to create visually engaging shots. Learn about things like depth of field and lighting techniques.

Buying a Consumer-Level Camera

When you search for a video camera make sure it has the following features:

- microphone input
- manual white balance control
- manual exposure control

- manual focus control
- manual audio control.

Microphone Input

Many cheaper cameras do not have a microphone input and rely on the built-in microphone. So keep searching until you find a model that has this input. Consumer cameras will almost always have unbalanced microphone inputs. (See chapter 6 for more details on balanced and unbalanced microphones.)

Manual White Balance Control

Your camera will most likely offer auto white balance—which will guess the white balance setting—or white balance presets for shooting indoors or outside in the sun. Don't settle for presets or automatic. Keep searching until you find a camera with manual white balance, which can dramatically improve video quality.

Manual Exposure

Setting the exposure levels of your video—how much light the camera lets in, which affects how light or dark your video is—is a personal preference. All professionals develop their own approach and style, and auto exposure robs you of that control.

Manual Focus

Your camera has no idea who or what you want to focus on, so it guesses by using the auto focus. Often it will get it right, but you shouldn't leave it to chance. Most models now offer a function called focus assist, which will help you get a sharper focus because it magnifies the image you are focusing on.

Manual Audio

Your camera should have manual audio control. This enables you to set the level once and ensure consistency throughout the recording.

Consumer Camera Accessories

You will also need some camera accessories to ensure professional shots:

- an external microphone
- a fluid head tripod with spirit level
- headphones
- SD card or recording media
- optional lighting kit.

External Microphone

The most common microphones used in video production are the shotgun and lavalier mic (Figure 11-1). If you are doing a lot of work on the run, a shotgun mic will be most versatile. If you are doing sit-down interviews or monologues, opt for a lavalier.

Figure 11-1. Shotgun and Lavalier Microphones

Shotgun microphones (left) are especially sensitive to noises directly in front of the mic and less so to sounds to the mic's side. Lavalier microphones (right) are ideal for conducting interviews and doing talking head shots.

Most lavalier mics, which are also referred to as lavs, lapels, and clip-ons, are omnidirectional. They are best when conducting interviews with one person. They have a very localized pickup pattern and can help reduce the noise of background sounds such as air conditioning because they focus more on sound in the immediate vicinity of the microphone.

Shotgun mics have a hyper cardioid pickup pattern, which means they mostly pick up sound that is directly in front of them. Sounds to the side are less pronounced. Cheaper shotguns, which cost less than $100, tend to be less discriminating than ones in the several-hundred-dollar range.

Fluid Head Tripod With Spirit Level

It's impossible to hold a consumer video camera very steady because it's so light. So you will need to buy a tripod to ensure your shots don't shake. A move every once in a while won't hurt, but if your shots are consistently shaky it will look unprofessional.

Your tripod will need a fluid head. Standard photography tripods don't allow for a smooth pan or tilt but a fluid head will. Make sure your tripod has a spirit level so you can set the camera level when shooting.

Headphones

You need a lightweight pair of comfortable headphones to hear what you are recording. Some cheaper cameras have miniature speakers built into them so you can listen to the audio if you play the recording back. But these are not good quality and headphones will be better. Also, you should listen as you record to be sure you get everything right the first time. Headphones with a cup on the earpiece will help isolate the recording from noise on location.

SD Card or Recording Media

It goes without saying that you'll need recording media for the video. Most cameras these days record onto SD cards. You'll need a ready stock of these, and a system to keep them labeled. It's also a good idea to buy a case for your SD cards to keep them safely in one place. An SD card holder costs less than $10 and prevents you having SD cards scattered around your desk, or lost somewhere in your desk drawer or at the bottom of your briefcase. If your camera still records onto magnetic tape, make sure you have plenty of tapes and a system for storing them.

Optional Lighting Kit

Lighting equipment represents an additional layer of complexity, which is beyond the scope of this book. We're concentrating on shooting in natural light. That said, the more light you have to shoot in, the better your picture quality. This is especially true for cheaper cameras. You can buy professional lighting kits, but cheap shop lights from home improvement stores can also do the trick when you're stuck with an impossibly low lighting situation.

Embedded Camera Accessories

If you plan to shoot on your smartphone or tablet, you should invest in a few accessories to improve video quality:

- external microphone
- headphones
- phone stand.

External Microphone

The need for an external microphone applies as much for smartphones and tablets as it does for consumer and professional cameras. There are many microphones available, but they need a special three-ring plug to work with your phone. When you buy your device, make sure it is compatible with your phone.

Shotgun microphones for smartphones can cost less than $50. They work well when you are shooting relatively close to your subject or sound. Likewise, lav mics for smartphones are even cheaper. If you are using a lav mic, make sure the cable is long enough. If it's only four or five feet, buy an extension, and make sure it's compatible with both your mic and phone.

Headphones

Make sure you have headphones to listen with while you record and when you play it back. Some microphone devices built for smartphones will provide an input for your headphones. If your device supports other types of headphones, like Bluetooth, you can use these, although they may drain the battery faster.

Phone Stand

Just as a camera needs a tripod, your phone needs a stand to ensure you don't end up with shaky video. Amazon has loads of choices—just check the size of your phone or tablet to be sure the stand will hold both its size and weight.

DSLR Camera Accessories

If you choose to shoot on a DSLR video camera consider adding these accessories to your video toolkit:

- tripod or stability control
- audio recorder
- lenses.

Tripod or Stability Control

If you choose not to shoot with a fluid head tripod, you can buy stability devices that mount your camera onto a brace that rests on your shoulder. These range from $200 to $1,000.

Audio Recorder

Most DSLR cameras offer audio capture. If yours doesn't you will need to purchase a digital audio recorder. Chapter 6 discussed audio recorders in more depth. Consider getting an external microphone for your digital recorder unless you can get the recorder close to the sound without it appearing in the shot. You can also use your cell phone and cell phone mic to record sound.

Lenses

The greatest advantage DSLR cameras offer over traditional video cameras is detachable lenses. Once you've got the hang of recording video on a normal lens, you may want to experiment with zoom and wide-angle lenses. Zoom lenses change the focal length of the lens. If this is done when the camera is recording, it will make the viewer feel as if he is moving closer to or away from the action. Wide-angle lenses capture more of the periphery of the scene and are helpful when shooting in small spaces. Zoom lenses used on DSLR cameras tend to be different than those traditionally used on video cameras. They are generally varifocal rather than parfocal, which affects the way you would set the focus, something we'll touch on in the next chapter.

Production Accessories

There are many accessories you can buy that will help you capture video. While you can do nicely with all we've mentioned so far, some of the following items can help you achieve certain effects.

Green Screen

Green screen—formally called chroma key—is a process in which someone talks in front of a green, or sometimes blue, backdrop and a computer replaces the green with a superimposed image. This is how weather forecasts on television have been broadcast for decades; the forecaster stands in front of a green screen and a computer replaces the green with a weather map.

You can buy a backdrop screen from most photographic retailers. The work of replacing the screen with another image is done with the editing software.

What's So Great About Green Screen?

I discourage folks from using green screen unless there's a very strong need. It takes longer to set up, is tricky in regard to lighting, and takes the computer longer to render. I've seen it waste more time than add value. One client shot a weekly motivational video in front of a green screen, presented by a senior vice president of his company. It would have taken him 10 minutes to take his camera down the corridor and shoot the video in the VP's office. But he insisted it be shot in front of his green screen. Unfortunately, the green screen was almost always improperly lit, which took more time to key, and it took more time to render the file. I couldn't see how the green screen made the video more effective or provided a narrative effect, because all he did was drop a generic office image behind him. But my client liked playing with technology.

Try not to fall into this trap. Don't use fancy effects and fun toys simply because you can. They take time and really should have a narrative purpose.

Teleprompter

If you have people talking to the camera, it may pay to invest in a teleprompter. You can buy a simple teleprompter for as little as $500, while professional models range into the thousands. Some models have screens built into them, while the cheaper models will work with your smartphone or tablet. If you use a teleprompter that requires a tablet or smartphone, you will need to download a teleprompter app to display the text. There are a number of free and premium options available.

Storyboard Apps

If you're not fond of drawing, you can download a storyboard app for your tablet or smartphone. These apps offer a range of objects and avatars you can use to block out your shots.

Drones

If you need bird's-eye shots, consider buying a drone. Perhaps you're creating an onboarding video and need an aerial shot of your campus. Maybe you're doing a video about geography. Drones range from a few hundred dollars to several thousand, but $500 can get you a good-quality drone with a mounted camera. More expensive drones have superior stability control and GPS devices to help you navigate.

Summary

When you buy video equipment, remember to look for the simplest product that will give you the manual functions you need. Don't start by looking for a brand you know; rather, start by looking for the camera that offers the features you need. Just make sure you don't go overboard on the features—many cameras are loaded with tools you really don't need and often they rob you of the control necessary to frame creative shots. Make sure your camera has a microphone input and manual functionality for white balance, exposure, focus, and audio. Buy an external microphone and a tripod to avoid "shaky cam." If you're using a device with an embedded camera, get hold of an external microphone to ensure crystal-clear sound. Once you have acquired your video gear, you need to go out and use it. Chapter 12 explores how to shoot professional-looking pictures for your videos.

Creating Video Content

In This Chapter
- How do you shoot video with manual and embedded cameras?
- How should you frame shots to draw the eye?
- What do you need to remember when shooting video?

For learning professionals, filming poor-quality shots is one of the biggest wastes of time. Your footage might be underexposed, have too much headroom, or just not work well with the other shots. While you can fix a lot of mistakes with your editing software, correcting video is time-consuming. Instead, you're better off getting your video right in the first place. For example, it should only take about 30 seconds to set the white balance on a camera, but if you forget, it will take several minutes to correct with editing software. Imagine if you forgot to set the white balance for 10 different shots? You could waste a lot of precious time.

Good shooting habits are often referred to as "shooting for the edit" because they make editing faster and easier. They also lead to better content. Here are four habits to develop that will get you better shots and save you time in editing:

1. **Only shoot footage that you need.** Excess footage slows you down, because you have more to sift through, and it takes up file space.
2. **Set up each shot carefully so it doesn't need to be corrected in the edit.** It is very common to waste time during the editing stage correcting simple mistakes that could have been avoided, such as incorrect white balance or underexposed shots.
3. **Shoot so your shots flow together.** Pictures need to work together to create a flow. This requires you to think about the continuity of what's in the picture and the movement in the picture.
4. **Look for additional cutaways.** Professional editors often bemoan the fact that they don't have enough shots to work with. When you are shooting, look out for additional elements beyond what you have in your storyboard so the editor can have additional material. Often, in the editing stage, you discover you need more than what you planned.

The tips and techniques shared in this chapter are based on these habits.

Shooting Video With Manual Function Cameras

Hopefully, you will be shooting on a camera with manual functions, for the reasons discussed in chapter 11. Here are five manual steps to set up the shot that should become habitual. To remember them, think of them as the five "-ites":

1. **Height:** Stabilize the camera to the right height.
2. **White:** Set the white balance.
3. **Light:** Set the exposure.
4. **Tight:** Set the focus.
5. **Bright:** Get good audio.

The pictures we show of these functions are based on a Canon Vixia. This is the cheapest camera on the market at the time of publishing that offers all the basic functions you need to have. I use this model in my workshops for people who want to make video fast on a low budget.

Height: Stabilize the Camera to the Right Height

Shaky cam is a sure sign of amateur video, but it's easily avoided by stabilizing the camera on a fixed object. The best object for this is the fluid head tripod. Tripods have three parts to adjust: the legs, spirit level, and release plate.

To set it to the right height, you need to extend the legs. When the legs are long enough, ensure the tripod is level. If you're on a slope, one or two legs may need to be different lengths. Use the spirit level to check if the tripod's head is level—it is level when the bubble is in the middle of the circle.

Figure 12-1. Spirit Level

In this image, the spirit level shows the bubble in the middle of the circle. This signifies that the tripod is level.

Next, attach your camera to the release plate. The release plate screws onto the base of your camera; depending on the model you have, it will then clip, click, or slide onto the head of your tripod. Make sure the release plate is screwed to your camera tightly so it doesn't shift. There is usually a stud in addition to the screw to lock your camera in place and prevent it from twisting.

Figure 12-2. Release Plate

The quick release plate screws onto the bottom of the camera. It is important to screw the plate on tightly so the camera doesn't move independently of the plate.

Now click the release plate into the tripod.

If you do not have a tripod, you can use a monopod. A monopod is a simple telescopic device that holds the camera. It has a folding foot platform for you to keep it steady. If you are traveling and can't get a tripod or monopod, use a stationary object to stabilize the camera, such as a wall or chair.

White: Set the White Balance

One of the biggest improvements in video quality that I see in my workshops is when people learn to use white balance, which refers to the color temperature of your shot. It dramatically improves the realism of your shots. There is some complex science behind white balance but in a nutshell, the color white, as you would see on a white piece of paper, looks different under different lighting conditions. If you looked at that piece of white paper under artificial light inside a building, it will appear slightly amber. But if you hold that same piece of paper outside under direct sunlight, it will appear slightly blue. The amazing thing about the human eye is it knows that the piece of paper really is white, so it will automatically adjust your brain's perception of the color white. The paper will thus look neither amber nor blue but white. It also adjusts the range of other colors in relation to this.

Cameras are not as sophisticated as your eyes. They see the white piece of paper, and indeed anything that is white, as slightly amber when filmed indoors and slightly blue when filmed outdoors. So if you have indoor and outdoor footage, the whites will look different in each shot, which creates discontinuity. These differences also affect the range of other colors, so all the colors will look slightly off.

To avoid this, whether you shoot indoors or outdoors, you need to tell the camera what true white is so it can adjust every color in the spectrum to look correct. If all this sounds confusing, don't worry. Once you start setting the white balance, you'll see how it makes sense on a practical level.

Most cameras offer auto white balance and some even have presets for indoor and outdoor lighting. It can be tempting to use the presets, but remember they are based on the color temperature in a typical room. Every room has different lighting so these presets are approximations. The best way to get correct white balance is to set it manually for the lighting conditions you are filming in.

White balance control is generally accessed through the camera's menu. Given that every camera has a different menu structure, you'll need to hunt through the menu or consult your user manual to find it.

Figure 12-3. White Balance Menu

The white balance control on most consumer cameras is accessed through the menu, by way of a touch screen.

When you set your camera to establish the correct white balance, hold a white piece of paper about five to 10 feet in front of it. If you don't have a white piece of paper, you might be able to find a white surface in the room such as a white wall or a whiteboard in a classroom. Zoom the camera in on the paper or wall so the viewfinder is filled with white. Now, press the white balance button. You'll see two little wedges flash as the camera works out the color temperature and sets all the colors of the camera. Once the two wedges stop blinking you are ready to go. Now zoom out and look at the picture.

Figure 12-4. White Balance Wedge

The camera indicates that the white balance is being set by flashing
the white balance icon, which can be seen in the middle of the screen.

Set the white balance whenever you move to a new lighting condition. If you're moving the camera around one room, you can set the white balance once; however, if you move to a different room or outside, you'll need to set it again.

Light: Set the Exposure

When it comes to lighting in video, you need to consider two things: Is there enough light in the environment you are shooting, and is the exposure set correctly?

Many consumer cameras do not work well in low light, so you may need to brighten the picture using the camera's exposure control. Some cameras will call this brightness, others exposure, and still others iris. Consumer cameras can struggle to increase the brightness and you will often find the picture looks grainy. The best way to avoid this is simply to shoot in situations with lots of light.

When you set up your shot, look for the main source of light, known as the keylight. The sun will most likely be your keylight when shooting outdoors during the day. Indoors, it could be the sun streaming through a window or a row of ceiling lights. Position the people or objects you are filming so the keylight shines on them. If you are filming a person, make sure there is plenty of light to illuminate the eyes. If shooting under office lights, stand at an angle to the overhead lights, rather than directly underneath, to avoid shadows in the eye socket, which obscure the eyes, and under the nose.

Figure 12-5. Good Lighting vs. Poor Lighting

Make sure the main lighting source is aimed toward the person in your shot. This will ensure that the person is clear and easy to see.

Do not shoot into the light, such as having someone stand in front of a window, because your subject could become a silhouette.

Make sure the light shines on your subject and you are not shooting into the light. A common mistake is to film a person standing in front of a window, when the window is really the keylight. Your subject ends up as a silhouette because it is behind the person and you are shooting directly into the light (Figure 12-5).

Once you have established a well-lit place to film, you need to set the camera's exposure. Lighting is quite a personal thing—you could talk to three different camera operators and find they all have their own approaches to setting the exposure. You will develop your own style over time. As you learn, the important goal is to ensure the shot is neither overexposed nor underexposed.

Overexposed shots look washed out and lose detail in the lighter areas. They are also very difficult to fix in the edit suite. Underexposed shots tends to obscure detail in areas where there are shadows. Sometimes they can be salvaged by editing software. A well-exposed shot will make the object or subject easy to see without causing viewers to strain their eyes (Figure 12-6).

Figure 12-6. Correct Exposure, Overexposure, and Underexposure

Correctly Exposed

Overexposed

Underexposed

Tight: Set Your Focus

Good video is well focused, meaning the object or subject in focus is sharp, not blurry. To focus a video camera, you need to set the focus when you are zoomed in tight on your subject (Figure 12-7). You will not have enough visual detail to set the focus if it is set on wide. Many cameras offer a function called focus assist. This magnifies the picture to give you more detail to help you make that picture nice and sharp. Depending on the camera model you use, you may find your camera automatically switches into focus assist mode. Check the manual for details.

So what should you zoom in on? If you're focusing on a person, zoom in on the eyes and adjust the focus until the eyelashes are sharp. Then zoom out. If you are shooting an inanimate object, focus on the part of the object that is either of most interest to the viewer or has sharper edges so you can more easily focus it.

Figure 12-7. Zoom In to Focus

You'll recall from the last chapter that DSLR lenses are generally varifocal rather than parfocal. Varifocal lenses do not hold the focus when zooming out. So if you are using a DSLR, you do not zoom in to focus; instead, you frame your shot and then set the focus at that point.

Bright: Setting Audio

Bright is an audio term used to describe audio recordings that sound crisp and clear. So we're borrowing that term to help remember the importance of good clear audio when shooting video. You need to do two things to capture good audio in your videos. The first is to choose the right microphone for your purpose and position it close to the sound source. The second is to adjust the audio levels on the camera.

We discussed microphones in chapter 6, particularly shotguns and lavaliers. Good audio is only possible when you get the microphone close to the sound. The further the mic is from your subject's mouth, the more the microphone will pick up ambient sounds like the HVAC and echo. If your camera is a long way from the person in shot, perhaps on the other side of the room, you will need a long cable to connect the camera to the microphone, which needs to be positioned close to the person's mouth. Shotgun mics allow a little more distance than lavaliers, but not much. Check the clarity of the recording in your headphones to gauge whether the mic is close enough.

Once your mic is well positioned, you will need to go into the camera's menu and set the audio levels. Cameras often default to auto controls so you'll need to set your camera's audio function to manual. It's important to set the audio level based both on what you hear through your headphones and what you see on your screen.

Your screen will show little bars that light up when they detect sound. These are called peak meters and display how loud your sound is, measured in decibels (db). When the audio goes over 0 db the audio will be clipped and sound distorted. Achieving the right level is a balance between avoiding clipping and being too low. To get the balance right, aim for an average reading of around −12 db. It's OK if you have an individual sound that occasionally hits −1 or 0, but keep most of the audio at −12 db.

Before you start recording your video, do a sound check in your headphones and ask the person speaking to talk for a minute or so. Use that to set the audio levels accordingly.

The 5 "-ites" of Camera Setup

1. Height: Set the tripod to the correct height and make sure it is level.
2. White: Set the manual white balance on your camera.
3. Light: Position your subject or object in the best lighting situation and set the manual exposure on your camera.
4. Tight: Zoom in tight and focus the picture.
5. Bright: Position your external microphone close to the sound, set the audio levels to average −12 db, and use headphones to check how it sounds.

Shooting Video With Embedded Cameras

If you are using a smartphone, tablet, or small flip-style camera, you will most likely be limited to working with auto functions. That means no direct control over white balance, exposure, focus, or audio levels. However, there are some techniques that can help you minimize these limitations.

Hold the Phone Correctly

Before we discuss ways of getting around auto functions, a quick comment on aspect ratio. Make sure you hold your phone so your video is captured at an aspect ratio of 16:9. Aspect ratio refers to the dimensions of the vertical and horizontal sides of the frame. In practice, it is most commonly used to tell you whether your video is widescreen or not. 16:9 is widescreen and 4:3 is traditional video.

Check your phone to be sure you are holding it correctly. When you look at the aspect ratio, you want the longer side to be horizontal. In photography terms, you are aiming for the picture to be shot in landscape (Figure 12-8). If the horizontal line is not longer, such as with portrait shots (Figure 12-9), you will have sidebars on the final video, which is distracting.

Figure 12-8. A Landscape Shot

Figure 12-9. A Portrait Shot

The only exception to this is when you are shooting video for social media sites that require the video to be in portrait. However, most learning management systems and video sites like YouTube and Vimeo will require a 16:9 aspect ratio.

Stabilize the Device

Just as you need to stabilize a standard camera, you also need to stabilize a phone or tablet when you shoot video. If you don't have a stand for your phone, hold the device with both hands to reduce the wobble.

Don't Use the Zoom Function

Most smartphone cameras do not have optical zoom lenses; they use digital zoom. Digital zoom leads to a more pixelated image with less detail. To get clear close-ups, ditch the digital zoom and then physically move your camera close to the person or object.

Use an External Microphone

Phone microphones have improved in quality but an external microphone will still make your video sound more professional. If you are unable to access an external microphone, physically move your device closer to the person so she is nearer the microphone. Without an external microphone, you should really only have close-ups when people are speaking; any further away and the quality will degrade dramatically.

Framing Shots

To achieve professional-looking video, you need to frame shots in a way that draws the eye. The rule of thirds is a visual art principle that has been used by artists and architects for millennia, as well as by photographers and cinematographers, to frame subjects in a visually stimulating way. Imagine the screen is divided into three vertical and horizontal sections, and imaginary lines separate each third. The rule suggests that you will make the picture more visually engaging if you place objects or people at one of the points where these lines intersect.

There are a number of theories to explain why this works. One theory relates to the change principle. Let's say you are shooting a talking head shot and position your talker in the center of the screen. It will appear uniform and symmetrical, which satisfies the brain so the viewer zones out. However, if you position the person's head on the right or left of the screen, it feels incomplete, creating uncertainty and the anticipation that something needs to happen, thus drawing the eye.

The rule of thirds suggests that you should position important people or objects at the top of the screen, centered on the line between the top two-thirds (Figure 12-10). This draws more attention than something placed on the lower part of the screen.

Figure 12-10. Rule of Thirds

Shots are more engaging when key elements of the picture, such as the eyes, are positioned at the intersection of the lines.

When you frame the shot symmetrically, such as positioning the person in the middle of the frame, it has less power.

When filming a face, position the person's eyes so he is on the line between the top two-thirds. Even if it crops the top of the person's head, viewers are more interested in the eyes than the hairstyle. A common mistake novice videographers often make is allowing too much space above a person's head. This is called headroom. Too much headroom makes the frame appear out of balance (Figure 12-11).

Figure 12-11. Example of Headroom

Headroom refers to the space on the screen above the head. Shots with too much headroom appear unbalanced and can make the subject appear diminished.

Another important consideration for framing shots is to allow what's known as looking space (Figure 12-12). If you follow the rule of thirds when filming someone, you will position the person on the left or right side of the screen, and he will most likely look either left or right. Depending on which side of the screen your subject is on, left or right means he looks at space on or off the screen. When he looks at space on the screen, he looks engaging. When he looks at space off the screen, it feels as if he has his back turned to the viewer. Unless you are deliberately creating the feel of aloofness or disengagement, frame your shot so people are looking onto the screen.

Figure 12-12. Example of Looking Space

When someone looks onto space on the screen, it feels more engaging.

When someone looks onto space that seemingly exists off the screen, it can feel as if the person is looking away from the viewer.

The Practice of Shooting

You've now worked through how to set up your shots. You've set the white balance, exposure, focus, and audio. The camera is sturdily mounted on the tripod. You've framed your shots so they draw the eye. What's next? Just press the red record button? Well, that's part of it, but there are still more tidbits that make editing easier.

Roll for 10

The term *roll for 10* comes from the days when cameras recorded video onto tape; it simply means to start recording the video 10 seconds before the action starts and switch it off 10 seconds after the action has finished.

When you press record, it takes the camera a few seconds to actually start recording. So, if you are filming someone walking past the camera and you hit the record button when the person starts walking, you will miss the first few seconds of the action. This causes problems for the editor because he will have to cut into the action after it has started, which will look abrupt. Starting earlier ensures you won't miss the beginning. It also offers a little extra breathing room when trimming your footage. By the same token, keep the camera rolling for 10 seconds after the action has finished. Some newer cameras have a function in which they are always recording, but discard the footage a few seconds later. So with these cameras, if you hit record, they will keep those previous few seconds before you hit start. However, entry-level cameras don't have this feature, so rolling for 10 is an important habit regardless.

Keep an Eye on Continuity

If you're following the three- or five-shot formula, you will be shooting the same action three or five times from different positions. It is really easy for the person in your shot, especially if she is not a professional actor, to repeat the action differently each time. For example, if you film her walking into a room and she puts her hand in her left pocket, she needs to put her hand in her left pocket for every other take as well. But this is easy to forget, so you must keep an eagle eye on continuity.

It's not just action that needs to be consistent. Keep an eye on what is in the background. If you're shooting action on the side of the road with intermittent traffic, you may have a truck roll by in the background in one shot and a school bus in the other. This makes the edit look very obvious and you won't be able to use the different shots.

Get Extra Cutaways

Before you start shooting, walk around and look for interesting objects or actions that relate to the topic. If you're doing a sales education video for a car dealer and filming on the sales lot, look for objects that are visually interesting but were unanticipated on the storyboard, such as the sale flags blowing in the breeze. Maybe you see a nice symmetry in the way the cars are parked. Perhaps you see some cars driving into the service bay. Even though they are not in your storyboard, shooting these extra shots will give you more options when editing.

Chapter 13 will discuss cutaways, often referred to as B-roll, in more detail. When transitioning between shots, you can hide the jump with these cutaways. And when a shot goes for too long, such as an interview, you can go to the cutaway so you have a shot change that keeps the viewer's attention. Cutaways are invaluable as backup in the editing process, so shoot as many of them as possible.

Shoot Action

Remember, it's important that you shoot video with action in it. If you find yourself shooting a storyboard that has lots of static images, shoot some extra takes that have action. For example, if your storyboard features a wide shot of the front door to a public building, get some people to walk through that front door. If you need to get a close-up of a door handle, get an additional close-up of someone turning that handle. Movement is much more engaging than static shots. Action draws eyeballs.

Safety: Film With Someone

When you shoot video, don't do it on your own. If you are doing your job well, all your attention will be focused on the viewfinder and action in front of you; you're not looking around. If you're dollying back during a shot, your eyes should not be on the ground behind you, which may be uneven or have microphone cables you could trip on. Likewise, if you're shooting in a public location, you would be unaware of someone who wants to pick your pocket. So plan to have someone work with you as a second set of eyes.

Summary

There's a lot to remember when capturing good shots. Developing the skills to get your shots right the first time takes time and practice, but is worth it. If you feel overwhelmed by all there is to learn, start by developing one skill at a time and gradually build up from it. When you shoot right the first time—setting white balance, exposure, focus, and audio correctly—you save a lot of time in the edit, the shots will be easier to bolt together, and your video will look awesome. And being conscious of continuity and framing your shots following the rule of thirds will make it more engaging and professional.

Editing Video Content

In This Chapter

- What is the best way to organize the video edit?
- What is the most efficient editing work flow?
- How do you cut all your shots together and transition between them?
- How do you incorporate video graphics and audio files?

Editors are the unsung heroes of video production. They take all the footage, which until this point is just a collection of disparate video files, and make it flow smoothly as a visual story. They then add music, sound effects, and graphics, along with visual and audio effects, to transform it into a complete visual learning experience.

Just as audio editing was originally a very physical process—cutting magnetic tape and joining it together—film editing used to be as well. The difference was that editors worked with celluloid, long strips of plastic film. And just as audio editing is now digital, video editing today is also performed with computer software, with the physical work limited to using a mouse and keyboard.

Editing Software

There are many editing programs available for both Mac and PC computers. Choosing one is a matter of finding what you are most comfortable using. Most packages offer really good features but use different work flows, so you should look for one that works for you. Download trial versions and explore which ones are easy and suit your mindset. The software you choose will not determine how good your video is. The editing decisions you make will.

Editing software is generally one of two types: storyboard or timeline. Storyboard editing packages allow you to import your video clips in order, and you simply trim them down by cutting out parts of the clips that are not needed. It's almost like working with PowerPoint. Timeline editors allow you to import the videos onto a timeline, which offers greater precision.

If you're only editing video once a month or less, you might be best served with a storyboard editor like Windows Movie Maker or Apple's iMovie. These are very quick and easy to learn—

iMovie is a little more complicated than Movie Maker, but still relatively straightforward. If you don't edit video very often, it's easy to forget the software, so you find yourself having to relearn it every time you edit. Storyboard packages will be quicker to relearn.

While editing programs with timelines offer more precision and functionality, they tend to be more complicated, with vast arrays of features that take time to learn. Adobe Premier and Sony Vegas are timeline-based. If you are going to edit video regularly, you won't have to keep relearning them, and you will also find that the added functionality enhances your control. Camtasia, which sits between software like Premier and Movie Maker regarding ease of use, is also timeline-based.

The craft of editing, which has evolved since the early days of cinema, follows a set of rules and conventions that make content quicker and easier to understand. Most factual videos, such as documentaries, news clips, and instructional videos, follow an approach known as continuity editing. Continuity editing aims to make a sequence of shots in a scene work together so the pictures flow naturally without any jarring disruption. Editors aim to re-create the action or scene in as realistic a way as possible. When camera positions, shot sizes, or camera angles change, the continuity approach ensures that the same people and objects are in each frame and that movement from shot to shot flows consistently.

Given the complexity of video editing, we're going to explore it first by looking at how to organize yourself for the edit, and then work through the steps you need to complete a video project. Then we'll explore some techniques to make your edits look professional, drawing on what's known as visual grammar.

Camtasia

This book takes an agnostic approach to software choice and errs toward easy-to-learn products that are affordable. Learning professionals don't have lots of time to invest in figuring out complex editing systems—they need to shoot, edit, and then move on to the next project. A lot of learning professionals use Camtasia, so we will illustrate the editing process visually with screenshots from Camtasia.

Organizing the Edit

Before you roll up your sleeves and start manipulating video files, it's important to get organized. Having a system for naming your files and a folder structure to keep them in order is crucial. It will save you time and allow you to direct more of your energy to the creative aspects of editing. Here are some thoughts you can adopt for or adapt to your work flow.

Naming Conventions

First, establish naming conventions for all your files. It matters less which convention you follow than the fact that you have one and adhere to it consistently. If you are in a team, having everyone consistently follow these file name conventions will make it easier for all of you to find content efficiently.

You could name video files based on the shot numbers in your script or shot plan, such as [Video Title]-[Shot Number]-[Take Number]. If you're creating a video on office conflict, the files might be named "officeconflict-15-3.mov." If you have more than one scene, you could add the scene number too. For production music, consider renaming your files based on their role in your video, such as [Video Title]-[Purpose]. It could be, "officeconflict1-intromusic.wav." When you rename production music files, keep notes so you can track them for copyright.

Alternatively, you could name the files for what's in the shot. This is helpful if you plan to use the footage again later. For example, you may use [Shot Size]-[Location]-[Season]-[Date]: "XWS-CustomerBuilding-Winter-Feb2016.mov." Why include the season? If you're using footage that was shot in winter in another video that features people in summer clothing, it will disrupt the continuity.

Folder Structure

Once you have file naming conventions, you should create a folder structure, as we discussed for audio. A video file system will be more complex than audio because you'll be pulling together audio, graphics, and video files. You'll find that you have so many files to keep track of that it can become a nightmare.

Here's one way to manage files for a video project, which is similar to what was suggested for audio in chapter 8. Create a new folder for each project and a subfolder for each episode if you are doing a series. Then create the following subfolders:

- **Footage folder:** This is for your video footage. For larger projects with more than 10 files, create subfolders to better manage different topics. It's up to you to decide how to divide them. Some editors will have a subfolder for each day of filming, while others may organize them around a topic. It's your choice.
- **Audio folder:** Keep your audio files here. If you have more than 10 files, consider further subfolders for different types of content such as music, sound effects, or voice-overs.
- **Graphics folder:** This folder is for the graphics you will use in your video. Again, if you have a lot of them, group them into further subfolders.
- **Project folder:** This is where you save your project file. You may find you have more than one project file because you are creating two versions of the same video—perhaps a short version and an extended one.
- **Final folder:** This is for the final exported video file. You may have several final files because you create a mobile and desktop version. Or you might have a version that is formatted to the specific requirements of your learning management system (LMS).

- **Admin folder:** This is your folder to save copyright details, artist releases, scripts, storyboards, and other documents you may need to reference during or after editing.

Some editing programs allow you to drag your media folders into the program to access from a project window. Some will rename your folders as *bins,* a term used back in the days of physically cutting film.

Saving Your Work

You will save two types of files when you edit video. One is the project file and the other is the final video file. The project file is a data file created by the editing software that has instructions for which shots will appear in your video, which parts of these shots you will use, at what point in time you will use them, and any effects that you apply to them. When you do the editing, the project file is updated. When you are finished, the editing software uses the data file to render all the shots, audio clips, and graphics into one final video file.

The project file does not contain video, only instructions on how to play it. So if you send a project file to your LMS administrator it will not play any video—it will be simply a set of data that makes no sense outside the world of your editing program. Every software program has its own proprietary file format for the project file. If you edit video in Premier, the project file will only work in Premier. It won't work in Camtasia or Vegas.

File Formats

Media files come in many shapes and sizes. You won't work with all of them, but here are the most common ones:

- **AVI:** Developed by Microsoft back in the early 1990s, AVI files tend to be very large. This file format plays on Macs and PCs.
- **WMV:** This is a compressed video file from Windows. WMVs are some of the smallest video files, but due to their small size picture quality isn't great.
- **MOV:** Known also as QuickTime files, MOVs were developed by Apple. You will need the QuickTime player or programs like VLC to play QuickTime videos on a PC. They tend to be high quality but have large file sizes.
- **FLV:** Known as Flash, this format was developed by Adobe and requires the Flash Player or Flash Plugin for web browsers. It is one of the standards for playing video over the web and is used by video publishers such as Hulu, Yahoo!, and Reuters.
- **MP4:** This format is technically known as MPEG-4 and can be compressed while maintaining reasonable picture quality. MP4 works with HTML5 and is becoming more popular than Flash video.

If you're uploading to YouTube or Vimeo, the recommended file format is MP4. However, your LMS administrator may require something different. Most editing software programs provide presets to make exporting easier. When rendering the final file you can select an option to render it for YouTube, Dailymotion, OneDrive, and so forth.

Video File Size

Video file sizes are much larger than other files we use on a day-to-day basis, like PDFs, documents, spreadsheets, podcasts, and graphics. The extra size makes video take longer to download or stream. To combat this, you need to compress the files, which reduces the size of the video by reducing its quality. This may compromise the quality of movement or remove detail from parts of the picture, making it appear grainy or more pixelated. Internet bandwidth continues to increase, so compression may not be as important one day. However, for now we need to be conscious of it. When you render your final video file, your editing package will compress the file size. There are a number of things you can do to aid the compression process and keep the file size small. Minimizing camera movements such as pans and tilts will help, as will opting for simple cuts rather than fancy transitions.

Establishing an Editing Work Flow

So, you've got your footage and you're ready to edit. What do you do and in what order? Editors tend to develop their own work flows based on how they like to work; you'll find that once you get into the rhythm of editing, you will establish a way that works for you.

To speed up the process of editing and reduce stress, it's important to start by organizing your files. When you are ready to work in your editing software, work first on your videos before bringing in supporting message layers like music and voice-overs. Then add effects. When everything is roughly in order, go back and fine-tune everything.

Let's get specific.

1. Import Video From Camera

The first task in editing is to import your shots from the camera onto your computer and save them in the footage subfolders in your project folder. It's important to edit media files from a location on your computer and not directly from the camera because if you disconnect the camera, your files go with it.

2. Import Supporting Media Files

You will now need to import the graphics and audio files and save them into the appropriate subfolder. The audio files may include music, sound effects, and voice-overs. It's not necessary to record voice-overs and create all your graphics before the editing starts. However, some people like to have everything ready so it all fits into place efficiently. Others prefer a little flexibility and like to wait before designing the graphics or recording voice-overs to see how the shots cut together. If you plan to create the graphics within your editing software, using the titling function, you won't import them at this stage. Whether to create graphics before editing or during is a matter of choice.

3. Rename Media Files

At this point, your video files will likely have filenames like "004.mov" or "009.mp4." These names were designed for the camera to keep track of the files. But they weren't designed to make it easy for you. So, rename each file according to your naming convention.

4. Review the Footage

It's tempting to start editing right away. But not so fast. If you start editing without reviewing your footage, you'll be editing shots based on how you remember shooting them. This is not as helpful as you might think because your memory is very different from what was actually recorded. You remember it as a three-dimensional experience involving all senses, but video only uses sight and sound, which is an entirely different experience. So to fully appreciate the videos and how they work narratively, set time aside to review the footage. The review is also a helpful opportunity to take notes about the shots and get a heads-up if anything is needed to correct them. For example, an underexposed shot may need to be brightened. It will also speed your decision-making process because you'll have a better sense of what shots you have to work with.

5. Create a New Project

Now that everything is ready to roll, it's time to open the editing program and create a new project. Some software will give you the option to specify project settings like video resolution and file type, whereas others will offer either default or recommended settings. Make your selection and save it into the project file subfolder. Now you're ready to start editing.

6. Import and Position Footage in Your Order

The first practical step after setting up your project file is to import your shots and any specific graphics files (such as text graphics) into the software and position them in the order they appear on the storyboard (Figure 13-1). Most editing packages use a timeline, so you would simply import or drag and drop them in so they run in order. Don't worry about getting the timing right just yet—you only need things in order. For more complex video you may choose to create several video tracks for cutaways and B-roll.

Figure 13-1. Video Shots on a Timeline

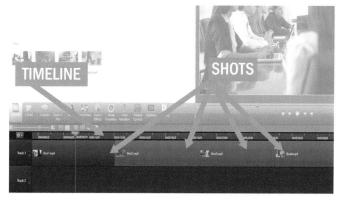

Each individual shot is positioned in sequence along the timeline.

7. Roughly Trim Each Shot

With each shot positioned in the order it will appear, cut out the bits of each shot you do not need and set the length of appearance for any graphics. If you "rolled for 10" when you shot the video, you'll have at least 10 seconds to cut out at the beginning. And you may want to cut from that first shot to the second halfway through the action. This process is called trimming because you are effectively trimming each shot, shortening it to the length it needs to be. Editing programs vary in how you trim each shot. In Camtasia, as in Figure 13-2, you simply place your cursor over the end of the shot, and with your left mouse button down, drag left or right until you have trimmed it to your desired point. As you trim each shot and it becomes shorter, you will move the shot along the timeline so it is next to the previous shot and runs from shot to shot without a break. At this point it doesn't matter if the changes are not smooth because you'll fine-tune everything later once other elements have been added.

Figure 13-2. Trimming a Shot in Camtasia

Each shot is trimmed to start and finish at the appropriate time, and to flow as a natural sequence.

8. Import Audio

Now that the visuals flow, it's time to add audio. Pictures carry most of the message, which is why we import and trim the pictures before other message layers. Now you can add music, sound effects, and voice-overs. Voice-overs can be recorded in your video editing program or using other programs like Audacity. If you use other programs, you would record the audio as a WAV or MP3 file and import it into the video editing software.

When you import audio, it will appear as a new track either above or beneath the video track. You will need to trim the audio to fit the pictures. In most editing programs, you can trim audio in much the same way as video.

At this point, your video is starting to take shape. This would be a good time to have your subject matter expert sign off on the accuracy of the visual content and spoken word. Remember, she can comment on style, but style is ultimately your domain. Only have her sign off on the accuracy.

9. Add Effects and Transitions

Editing programs offer a host of effects and transitions; now that the message layers are roughly in place, it's time to add these effects. You might need to adjust the brightness and contrast of one shot, add a sepia tone effect to another, or drop in a new background using chroma key. The transition could be a dissolve or wipe. It can be tempting to add effects and transitions earlier in the process, such as while you are trimming the shots. However, it's more efficient to add them all at the same time while the effects dialog box is open. Otherwise, you'll be opening and closing the dialog box multiple times while you trim. Doing all the effects at once—such as ensuring all the dissolves are of the same length and conform to the general style of your video—also helps you stay consistent.

10. Fine-Tune Your Edits

By now, your media assets will have been assembled in order and be roughly finished. However, there will be things to fine-tune. Perhaps it's a transition that was too abrupt or broke continuity. Maybe you need to extend the length of a shot to accommodate an extra bar of music. This stage is where you smooth out any kinks. Once this is done, watch the video. Once you're happy with it, send it to your SME to sign off the accuracy if you haven't already.

11. Export the Video

Once the video is complete, it's time to render it into a final video file. This is where your software will combine all the different media files (audio, video, and graphics) to make one complete media file that you can upload to a video-sharing site or LMS, or save to your hard drive and use in classrooms.

Cutting Your Video

In his book, *In the Blink of an Eye,* editing guru Walter Murch concedes that a basic purpose of editing is "cutting out the bad bits." If you're editing an interview with a subject matter expert, you will cut out anything that does not relate to the learning objective. You might need just five minutes of the half-hour recording. Cutting out so much material can present problems and make your edits look unnatural, leading to what's known as a jump cut.

A jump cut occurs when you cut from one shot to another in the middle of the action, and some of the flow is disrupted. Let's say you are shooting a scene where a woman takes a handkerchief out of her purse and blows her noise. To make it more visually interesting, you might have shot two takes, a wide shot from the front and a mid shot from the side. Let's say you cut from the wide shot as she pulls her hand out of the purse and then cut to the mid shot at the point she blows her nose. Five seconds of time have just disappeared—the time it took for her to raise her hand from the purse to her nose. The gap in time breaks the flow and feels awkward. Visually, the picture jumped five seconds, hence why they are called jump cuts. You need to either avoid jump cuts or hide them.

If you cut out parts of an interview with your subject matter expert, you will have lots of jump cuts that disrupt the flow. One method of hiding jump cuts is to use cutaways. This is common practice in news and documentary making. Where you have a jump cut, you overlay another shot to distract the viewer from the natural flow. This shot could illustrate what the subject matter expert is talking about or simply show a different angle or related piece of visuals. If the subject matter expert is explaining how computers work, you may have a picture of someone tapping away on a computer. Or, you could cut to a close-up of him moving his hands. You'll recall in chapter 12 that we discussed the importance of getting extra shots for cutaways such as gestures.

There will be times you have an action shot that goes too long but is too important to delete. For example, a man walking down a street to knock on the front door of a house, which might take

30 seconds. You can reduce this from 30 to eight seconds by inserting a cutaway. Let's assume you shot the action following the three-shot formula: a wide shot of the whole street, a close-up of a nameplate that displays the street number, and a mid shot of him knocking on the door. The first two seconds could feature the wide shot of him walking down the street. Then you could cut to the close-up of the letterbox that shows the street number, then cut to the mid shot of him knocking on the door. You could then cut back to the wide shot showing him waiting at the door as it opens.

When you work with action shots, cut on the action. Let's say you're showing someone how to change the tire on a car. To make it interesting, you shoot both a wide shot of the front of the car while an actor bends down to place the jack under the car and a mid shot of the actor from the side as he places the jack under the car. The wide shot creates anticipation of what's going to happen and establishes the scene. If you wait until the actor has finished bending down in the wide shot to cut to the mid shot, it will lose momentum and create a jump cut. So the key is to cut from the wide shot to the mid shot during the action. Some editors plan for the cut to take place a third of the way through the first shot, with the remaining two-thirds of the action taking place in the second shot. It's not always as clear cut as that, so you will need to use your discretion.

Transitioning Between Cuts

The most practical task you will perform when editing is trimming shots; that is, determining where one shot ends and the next one starts.

Editors use a range of transitions to flow from one shot to the next. These are the most common:

- **Standard Cut:** This is simply where one shot stops and the next one starts.
- **Dissolve:** Also known as a cross-fade or mix, a shot fades out as the next shot fades in. Or at the end of a sequence, the shot fades to black.
- **Wipe:** This is where the next shot slides in over the former shot, often right to left or left to right.

The standard cut is very functional. In most cases it works best because it doesn't draw attention to itself unless the cut occurs in the wrong place. It works well for video streamed over the Internet because there is less transitional detail than dissolves and wipes, which can increase file sizes and appear jerky during playback. So it's good to stick to cuts if your video will be viewed over the Internet, unless that transition is necessary for carrying part of the narrative. For example, a dissolve can convey a flashback and manipulate the viewer's sense of time. Dissolves also carry an artistic quality, pacing the viewer's mood. A wipe can also help communicate flashbacks or changes in time, but it feels more businesslike and has less emotional and artistic qualities.

Video editing software packages offer many different effects for transitions that range from the simple cut to kitsch transitions like starbursts and keyhole bursts. Unless there is a narrative purpose to use a wipe or dissolve, it's best to avoid them.

Inserting Video Graphics

You'll find yourself creating different kinds of graphics for your video, including text graphics and captions. We consider what makes good graphics in more detail in chapter 14, which has been written by design guru Connie Malamed.

Text graphics are useful for reinforcing key learning messages. They also provide visual changes to keep viewers interested. You can generate text graphics with Photoshop, within the editing software, or in slide programs like PowerPoint or Keynote. Photoshop offers a lot of control and will provide you with high-resolution images, but using it can be time-consuming. Editing software programs are quick and easy but give you less control over the aesthetics than Photoshop. Slide programs, the happy medium, are generally easy to use and control. Simply create all your text graphics at once in PowerPoint and export them as GIFs or JPGs.

Text graphics should follow the rule of thirds and be as simple as you can make them. Avoid busy background textures and use as few words as possible. Strong sans serif fonts work well because they are easier to read. Make sure there is strong contrast between the background and the text itself. Hold the text graphic on the screen for as long as it takes the average person to read it two and a half times.

Captions, also known as lower thirds and Astons, are forms of text you can overlay to provide information such as the name and title of a subject matter expert or the time and location of the picture. Use colors that contrast with the background. If you have white captions, and the picture behind is light, use drop shadow to make the captions stand out. Use fonts that are strong and easy to read—sans serif fonts like Ariel Bold or Franklin work well.

Captions are generally positioned in the lower third of the screen. There are varying opinions about whether they should be left or right, but I think it's best to locate them at the lower right because that's where the viewer's eyes end up. As with text graphics, hold the caption for as long as it takes to read it two and a half times.

Adding Audio

While video is a picture-led modality, audio still plays an important role. In fact, you can make a few simple mistakes in your picture editing and very few people will notice. But poor audio will stand out like a sore thumb.

A lot of audio is music. Be careful when setting the volume of the background music because it can overshadow spoken word content. A lot of people struggle with hearing issues and find it difficult to distinguish between music and voice. So keep background music as soft as you can without it being inaudible.

If your video content is shorter than the music content, fade the music so it doesn't end abruptly. You can also edit music so it finishes at the same time as the video. This makes video look very polished, but takes some practice.

Many editing programs will give you audio compression and graphic equalizer controls. Using these functions will make your audio pop and sound professional. The settings for these are the same as audio, so check out chapter 8 for a recap.

Summary

The editing stage of video production is where everything comes together as a complete, polished package. If you feel a little overwhelmed by all you have to do, take heart. The best way to learn editing is to fire up the software and start playing. As you pick up techniques, you'll find that the process is quite fun.

This chapter is deliberately vague about how to perform some of these actions because editing software can approach tasks like trimming differently. That's why we focused on the craft more than the software. You can find how-to videos online for just about every software program available.

Today's software gives you much more control than film editors had when they were cutting celluloid. But despite all the bells and whistles, good editing is not about fancy transitions or special effects. It's about the content, and the editor's chief responsibility is to cut pictures together in a way that engages the viewer and conveys the learning objective.

Graphics and Learning

By Connie Malamed

In This Chapter

- What are the benefits of using graphics for learning?
- What does the graphic planning process look like?
- How do you select graphics?
- How do you edit graphics?
- Where do you place your graphics?

We are visual beings. For those who are sighted, the brain uses more resources for visual processing than for any other sense, more than hearing, smelling, and tasting. The optic nerve is packed with more than 1 million nerve fibers, taking in and sending information from the eyes to the brain. Most important to learning, we select and interpret this information without much conscious effort.

You may recall from chapter 9 that visuals in the video modality hold enormous power as a vehicle for learning. Perhaps that's because seeing is believing. When a friend or co-worker finishes a fantastical story with "I saw it," we tend to believe it. Going beyond video, this phenomenon lends itself to the believability of pictures, graphics, and the like. When we see a photograph in a newspaper or presentation slide, we believe the information to be more credible. Thus, adding relevant graphics to text-based learning content can strengthen the quality and effectiveness of your training programs.

Benefits of Graphics in Learning

Can you leverage the brain's impressive visual capabilities to improve instructional materials? As you might expect, the answer is yes. In the following, you'll discover five powerful benefits of using visuals in instructional materials, rather than using text alone.

Graphics Capture Attention

Gaining attention is one of the key ingredients of successful learning materials, and graphics are magnets for the eyes. Graphics draw the learner into your content. When looking at webpages, newspaper ads, and information brochures, readers tend to look at the pictures first. Think about the last time you were handed a workbook at a training program. While waiting for the session to kick off, you may have flipped through the workbook, zooming past pages of words. But when you came across a graphic, you stopped on that page to take a look. It stood out, whether it was an image, diagram, chart, or photograph.

Graphics Communicate Quickly

When compared with words alone, graphics are processed more quickly. Words must be read in a serial fashion, one after the other. In contrast, when you first look at a picture, you see it as one entity. If the graphic is effective, this holistic perception quickly gives you a sense of what the image is about.

Certain types of graphics communicate information more quickly than others. Icons, symbols, and silhouettes are reduced to the bare minimum of visual features necessary to be understood quickly.

Relevant Graphics Enhance Recall

When people encode information into memory, they often remember the text along with the meaningful pictures that accompany it. Remembering pictures and text together can aid the recall of information. Graphics may provide another communication channel and an additional connection for storing information in memory.

Graphics Improve Comprehension

Visuals have been shown to facilitate comprehension. They can depict interrelations between ideas and concepts, show spatial relationships in diagrams, and elaborate on how things work using arrows and other symbols. For example, data visualizations help people understand large amounts of quantitative information that would be difficult to manage otherwise.

Graphics Evoke Emotions

It is now well known that emotions are an important component of learning. Evoking emotions helps to maintain attention and makes content more meaningful and memorable. Graphics designed to evoke emotions, such as those that accompany a story or support statistics, are likely to move the learner more than words alone. Graphics bring your learning content to life.

The Graphic Planning Process

You can use the rapid media technique (plan, create, and edit) to develop graphics quickly and affordably, although you will need an additional, equally important, step at the end. This final step involves the placement of your graphics—identifying where to position them in a composition.

The goal of using a plan, create, and edit, place process is to ensure that your graphics are designed with intention rather than randomly or accidentally. Intentional design results in professional-looking materials that are more effective for learning.

Plan at Two Levels

To ensure that graphic design doesn't become an overwhelming task, start with a planning mindset. Think of graphic design as a problem-solving exercise. What is the problem? At the highest level, you must find a coherent visual treatment for a set of instructional materials. Answering this question will help govern the entire design and development process.

Planning a coherent visual treatment means choosing a color palette, one or two contrasting fonts, and an image style that is consistent throughout your materials. As the treatment evolves, you will find other aspects that you need to plan, such as designing layouts that work for different learning tasks.

Ultimately, when you plan for graphics, you do so at two levels. The highest or global level refers to the big picture perspective. The detailed level involves designing for individual units, such as pages or slides.

The Global Level

The advantage of planning at the highest level is that it creates some uniformity between every page, screen, or slide of your materials. Consistency (without being boring or redundant) makes your work not only professional, but also easier and faster for learners to decode because it looks familiar.

To design your overall visual approach, think through the following questions as they apply to the entire project:

- What visual approach will align with the audience, content, and overall purpose of the learning event?
- What visual approach and style will best communicate your message?
- What visual approach will represent the organization or institution for which you are developing the materials?
- What visual approach will embody novelty? What approach will surprise and delight the learner?
- If applicable, what visual approach will improve the user experience?
- What is my budget for graphics?
- What is the timeframe in which graphics need to be completed?

The Detailed Level

You will also need to plan which graphics will fulfill individual learning objectives and specific chunks of information. To select or create graphics for individual learning objectives, think through these questions:

- What type of graphic will best fulfill this learning objective?
- What graphic will enhance the application of knowledge and skills for this specific chunk of content?
- What graphic will influence a person to change her attitude?
- Is the graphic style consistent with the rest of the course?

You Have Many Style Choices

Have you noticed that many instructional materials rely on photographic images for their graphics? Although photographs are not inherently a poor choice, you need not limit yourself to this one style if it doesn't meet your needs. Part of planning involves finding the style that will be most effective in fulfilling your learning objectives and the message you want to communicate. So be sure to consider the appropriateness and feasibility of a range of graphic styles before deciding on one. If your materials look unique in some way, they are more likely to capture and maintain attention and to be remembered.

You may need to select more than one style. For example, if you need characters to tell a story but you also need to create information graphics, you will most likely want to use two different types of graphics: photographs or illustrations for the story, and diagrams, icons, or graphs for the information graphics. What follows is an explanation of different graphic styles to consider.

Photographs

Photographs are an obvious choice because stock photo agencies and websites offer millions of photographs, both paid and free. It is also fairly easy, with some planning, to shoot your own photographs. Use photographs when you need to show realistic images, if your time and budget are limited, or if you want to stress the credibility of your content. Consider black and white photographs to depict historical times, or for an artistic approach. Photographs can demonstrate actions, show what objects look like, and support the text.

3-D Graphics

Specialists in 3-D graphics create wireframe models on a computer, which then renders each model with a surface texture and lighting. The advantage of 3-D graphics is that they exist as objects that can be rotated and viewed from different angles. You can purchase 3-D graphics online or hire a 3-D artist to create them. They are ideal for showing pristine versions of objects and systems without the extraneous visual information included in photographs.

When your instructional materials require a visual explanation for clarity, consider 3-D graphics to represent technical, scientific, and medical subjects. You can also use 3-D graphics to visualize fantastical environments and characters in stories that motivate learners.

Illustrations

Illustrators either create images using drawing software or draw images by hand and digitize them with a scanner. The range of illustrated graphics is tremendous, from realistic renderings to cartoonish clip art and everything in between. Use illustrations when you are looking for a unique and expressive visual style to convey abstract concepts or humorous situations and characters. Like 3-D graphics, illustrations are also a good choice for depicting objects and scenes that are not visible to the unaided eye, such as comparing planets in the solar system.

Silhouettes

Silhouettes are subtle graphics that simply show the filled-in shape of an object or person without the details. They suggest a concept or topic without distracting the learner with extraneous information. As a graphic style, silhouettes can quickly communicate information.

You can often use silhouettes as an accompaniment to text. For example, in a safety lesson for construction workers, the silhouette of a person wearing protective gear could be placed next to the lesson text.

Icons

Icons are highly distilled graphics. When easily recognizable, icons are perceived and understood rapidly because there is less information to process than in a more detailed graphic. There are many creative ways to use icons, such as to:

- Represent data in information graphics.
- Represent categories of content.
- Guide navigation when placed on buttons.
- Replace bullet points.

Information Graphics

Information graphics, such as diagrams, graphs, and timelines, condense information and make it more concrete. Use information graphics to explain abstract or complex concepts. Diagrams are useful for representing systems and flow. Graphs are an excellent way to visualize and organize data into a comprehensible format. Timelines depict chronological content, including storytelling.

Well-designed information graphics make content easier to comprehend because the structure and layout of the visual often provides meaning. For example, it is easy to understand a company's structure by viewing a hierarchical diagram. Representing the steps of a cyclical process in a circular layout adds clarity to the concept.

Match Your Graphic to the Learning Goal

When planning graphics, think in terms of what style or format will match your goal. Then try to remain consistent throughout the materials in terms of the graphic style you choose to fulfill each goal. What follows is a list of common instructional and information goals and a corresponding graphic style (Table 14-1).

Table 14-1. Common Learning Goals and Graphic Styles

Learning Goal	Graphic Styles to Consider
Represent concrete objects	Photographs, 3-D graphics, illustrations, or icons
Tell a story	Sequence of photos or illustrations or a timeline
Persuade learners	Photographs to evoke emotions or graphs to visualize data
Explain complex concepts and show relationships	Visual metaphors or diagrams
Demonstrate a procedure or explain a process	Sequence of photos or illustrations to show the steps
Point out a relevant element in a graphic	Visual cue like an arrow or highlight
Depict components of a system	Labeled diagram of the structure
Make quantitative comparisons	A bar graph, pictograph, or line graph with multiple lines

Selecting Graphics

Once you have identified your overall graphic approach as well as the individual graphics you need to facilitate learning, you are ready to start selecting your graphics.

You may already be familiar with the many stock photo websites available. Stock photos are professionally shot images that are available for purchase with various licenses. Some sites offer free images, often with the stipulation that you credit the photographer. Other sites require you to pay per image or buy a set number of credits, which you can put toward acquiring images you need. On commercial stock photo sites, you can often find much more than photographs, such as illustrations, icons, silhouettes, information graphics, and other media.

When selecting graphics, seek out images that not only meet the instructional goals, but also are compelling to the learner. Here are a few guidelines:

- Select graphics that will be meaningful to the audience.

- Seek graphics that are inclusive and reflect diversity in race, age, ethnicity, disability, and gender.
- Search for graphics that are a bit unusual, rather than the typical stock photo showing a person smiling at the camera.
- Look for graphics that will evoke emotions when appropriate.
- Remember the wide range of graphic styles available.

Editing Graphics

Similar to how you correct and modify the written word, visuals also need adjustments to improve their quality and best meet the instructional goals. Photographs are the most likely—but not the only—type of graphic that will need editing. You will need to use graphic editing software, like Photoshop, GIMP, or a free online tool, to edit your images. PowerPoint is another option. Always save the edited file with a new name so that you have a copy of the original graphic if you need it for future use.

The first step of the editing process is to review the purpose of the graphic. Why did you select it? Then determine whether modifications will help you meet your goals. For example, a photograph may be too dark, or it may include too much information. An icon might need a color change or a background shape so that it stands out.

Some editing techniques that will give your visuals maximum impact are cropping, adjusting brightness and contrast, merging two images to create a new one, and resizing. Let's look more closely at these four editing tasks.

Cropping

No other editing technique may have a greater effect on a graphic than cropping. Cropping involves cutting away unnecessary visual information from a picture so that it has a greater focus. What remains is the essence of the image.

Stock photographs may be shot from a perspective that is different from your own. A photograph of a factory might show the entire production line, when what you need is a close-up of hands doing work. Or you may have an image of two people consoling someone who is upset when all you need is a close-up of the person in distress. When you trim away the distracting clutter, you create more meaning for the learner.

When cropping, consider the rule of thirds, which is effective for graphics as well as video. By dividing an image into thirds both horizontally and vertically, you can crop it so that the subject is aligned with one of the intersecting lines. This often makes your image more appealing to viewers. See chapter 12 for a more detailed discussion of the rule of thirds.

Adjusting Brightness and Contrast

You may have some images that appear dull and washed out, and you want them to have more punch. During the editing process, you can gently adjust the brightness and contrast to give the image a richer tone. Conversely, some images are too bright, or have too many stark shadows. You can reduce the contrast to even things out.

Suppose you were creating materials for a course on animal care for veterinary technicians. The photographs are critical to the content, but it is difficult to see how the technician is holding the animal in some of the images. By bringing the photos into a graphic editor, you can adjust the contrast so that the technician's hands can be seen more easily. This type of edit enhances the value of the photos to the learning experience.

Merging Two Images

Another powerful editing technique is to cut out a person or object and place it over a background image. This is one way to place people in new environments without conducting a photo shoot. For example, you can overlay a photo of a doctor onto a background image of a hospital corridor or overlay a photo of a child onto a background image of a playground. Merging two images in this way gives you more options to support the content, particularly when you can't find or don't have the budget for the graphics your materials require.

When merging images, a little technical knowledge goes a long way. A basic rule is to save the cut out image as a PNG file so it will maintain its transparent background. This allows the new background graphic to show through. You can also purchase stock photos of people with transparent backgrounds from publishers that specialize in graphics for e-learning.

Resizing and Resolution

The last phase of editing is to resize the graphic and adjust the resolution, as needed. The rule of thumb for resizing a graphic is to make it the size you need rather than accepting it as is. If you only need a small photograph, then reduce the size of the image in a graphic editor. This will reduce the size of the file, which is important if it will be viewed on the web. Smaller file sizes load more quickly, which avoids the frustration that learners experience when they have to wait for large files to display online. Also, avoid trying to enlarge a photo that is too small. This can result in a blurry image.

In addition to sizing, you may want to adjust the resolution of a graphic. Resolution refers to the details of an image expressed in dots per inch (DPI). A higher resolution will show more detail and have more dots per inch. Graphics for the Internet should be a lower resolution than graphics for print. This is because a lower resolution creates a smaller file size that will load quickly when displayed in a web browser or mobile device.

Most stock photo sites will list the DPI of a graphic. Select the DPI that is appropriate for where the image will be displayed. A 72 DPI or slightly higher image is suitable for the web and 300 DPI is suitable for print.

Once you've selected your graphics and edited them to suit your quality standards and instructional purpose, you need to figure out where to place them in the learning materials. This next section looks at some of your options.

Placing Graphics

Why should you be concerned about where a graphic is placed in your learning materials? An effective and pleasing arrangement of graphics and text provides certain benefits to your final product. A successful layout will:

- Provide a professional and polished look.
- Make it easier to comprehend the information.
- Indicate what is most important.
- Facilitate learning.

You can improve the layout of your designs in many ways. Four ways that can have a big impact are creating a balanced layout, using ample white space, establishing a visual hierarchy, and grouping related elements.

Create a Balanced Layout

Two common layout arrangements to consider for your designs are symmetrical and asymmetrical. A symmetrical layout refers to organizing the visual elements so they are centered in such a way that the left side is nearly a mirror image of the right side or the top is nearly a mirror image of the bottom. It does not have to be exact, but is close enough for the symmetry to stand out.

A symmetrical layout emanates balance and harmony because one side is equal in weight to the other. It is a neat and ordered approach to design. This orderliness makes the visual elements easy to perceive and process. A symmetrical design is not difficult to implement when there are just a few visual elements involved. But as the requirements get more complex, it is more difficult to maintain the symmetry. Use a symmetrical layout when you want a more formal and static design, and when you only have to place a few elements (Figure 14-1).

Figure 14-1. Example of a Symmetrical Layout

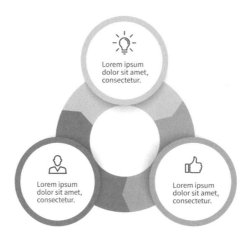

Conversely, an asymmetrical layout has varied elements on either side of the vertical or horizontal axis. This type of design is usually more dynamic than the symmetrical layout because it conveys a sense of disorder or tension. Because of this, viewers often find an asymmetrical layout compelling.

You can find balance in an asymmetrical layout by placing visual elements of equal weight on opposing sides of an axis. For example, you can balance a large image on the left with a large paragraph of text on the right. In this way, you create a sense of dynamic balance within a less stable arrangement. Use an asymmetrical layout if you have many elements to place or if you are looking for a dynamic and energetic design (Figure 14-2).

Figure 14-2. Example of an Asymmetrical Layout

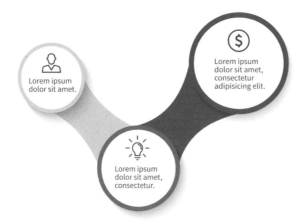

There are no strict rules for determining which layout to use for learning experience design. Rather, think in terms of aligning your design with the attributes of the audience, the content, and the personality that the organization wants to project.

Use Ample White Space

When looking at a visual, viewers tend to see an image or shape as the foreground and the empty space as the background. It may seem unintuitive to care about the empty space in a layout, yet this region is as important as the filled space. The empty space, referred to as white space in art and design, provides a place for the eyes to rest. It allows a visual to have breathing room. Providing sufficient white space in a layout makes it easier for a learner to visually scan and apprehend the materials without getting overwhelmed. Using ample white space is also a way to point out what is important because an image or text will contrast with the empty space. Note that white space can be any color.

The best way to work with white space is to try to see it as its own form. Examine the shape that the white space creates. Is it aesthetically pleasing? Is there a balance between white space and the visual elements? If you discover that the white space is broken into too many unrelated areas, adjust your layout. Often the solution is to remove elements rather than to add them.

White Space

Easy ways to provide white space in your designs:
- Use wide margins.
- Place padding around each visual element.
- Add a little more space between lines of text and paragraphs.
- Remove visual elements that are extraneous to your instructional message.
- Consider using one large image rather than many smaller ones.

Create a Visual Hierarchy

In addition to providing ample white space, you can facilitate learning by establishing a visual hierarchy. This influences the order in which a person sees and thus interprets the visual elements. It can also intentionally direct the learner's eyes to what is most important in your materials. A visual hierarchy can improve the efficiency of an instructional experience, helping learners to quickly find what is most relevant. Here are some of the many ways to achieve a hierarchy of emphasis.

Position

Researchers from the fields of user experience, educational psychology, and advertising report that a person's eyes first land on a page or screen in the upper left. Therefore, position the most important information at the top or left or both.

Size

Make the most important image or text the largest visual element in comparison to the others. You can also deemphasize the less important parts by making them smaller. Use a bit of restraint so that the size differences make sense but are not too extreme, unless done intentionally.

Color

Viewers will notice bright colors before they notice dull colors. Use vivid colors to bring the most important element to the top of the visual hierarchy. Then use calmer colors for the remainder of the design. What can you do if you want emphasis without color, such as when using text? If you want to emphasize a headline or a title that is displayed in black text, make it boldface or select a font with thick, heavy letters.

Visual Cues

You can direct the viewer's eyes to specific information by adding explicit visual cues:

- Add an arrow that points directly to the location where you want the viewer's eyes to land.
- Use a highlight in a contrasting color or spotlight to emphasize what is most significant.
- Place a photograph of a person looking directly at the most important information. This will guide the learner's eyes to the focal point because people are programmed to follow the eyes of another person.

Group to Show Relationships

When people look at a graphic, they tend to see the groups before seeing the individual parts. Also, viewers understand that items that are grouped together are associated with one another. For example, when you see a cluster of overlapping images, you assume they have some type of relationship.

Visual grouping is one of the strongest ways to impart meaning in a design. This principle should influence where you place various elements. If elements are related, place them in close proximity. The learner will process these elements as though they are associated. If elements are not related, place them at a distance from one another.

Summary

With practice, you will become competent in designing graphics. Rather than immediately jumping in to graphic selection, step back and think through your instructional goals. Then follow the plan, create, edit, place process described in this chapter. Designing with intention will result in a quality finished product that ultimately complements and enhances the other elements of your learning materials.

Graphics offer immense potential to transfer knowledge from the learning professional or subject matter expert to the individual learner. If you follow the work flow presented in this chapter, you'll be on your way to developing high-quality graphics without breaking your budget or wasting precious hours fumbling with complex software.

Screen Text and Learning

In This Chapter
- How do learning professionals use screen text in learning?
- How do learners behave when reading screen text?
- What are the screen text challenges for learning professionals?

The written word has been a key tool for learning professionals for what seems forever, whether it was the set of words chalked up on a blackboard that students hastily jotted in notebooks or handouts distributed in class. Text has provided trainers with a tool to share content for hundreds of years. And most learning professionals have a pretty good handle on how to write. Even if they're not consciously following the traditional rules of grammar, most will instinctively incorporate the classic principles of writing complete sentences, spelling words correctly, and using accepted punctuation.

This should not be surprising given you were taught the basics of English grammar when you were in school. If you learned a foreign language, you may have gone into it in more depth. So when it comes to writing text viewed by learners on a screen, such as their phone, tablet, or desktop computer, learning professionals should be well prepared, right? Maybe. But possibly not.

When creating text that will appear on a screen, it's important to remember the digital mindsets discussed in chapter 2, especially the second, being platform sensitive. Just as the video viewing experience is different in the cinema than it is on a phone, the experience of reading text on a screen is different than it is on paper. For example, text on paper is viewed under reflected light, while screens are backlit. Paper generally has a much higher resolution than the average screen, and while that is changing as technology advances, it will be some time before screens really reach paper resolutions. There are many different screen sizes as well—text viewed on a desktop computer monitor is different from text viewed on an iPhone.

So do the rules of writing printed text apply to screen text? To answer that question, we need to ask another question, one that should be the mantra of every media practitioner: Do these rules make text quick and easy to understand? Many rules of traditional grammar apply to screens because they make the content quicker and easier to understand. Other good practices, like avoiding tautologies and being consistent with tense, naturally help. But some don't. For example, using a sentence fragment instead of a complete sentence, or opting for super short paragraphs, will often make your screen text quicker and easier to understand.

Chapter 2 also discussed a number of universal media principles, including the need to keep everything short. For screen text, that means short words, sentences, and paragraphs. Media content needs to be simple, which for text translates to things like keeping just one idea in each sentence and paragraph, and avoiding the temptation to cram more than one learning objective into 300 words. Familiarity is important too. Words should be easy to recognize; don't use jargon. And it's important to keep content interesting by changing the way it's presented. For screen text, that means considering how learners engage with it and its visual impact.

Reading Behaviors

If there's one word to describe the mindset of the typical person reading web text, it might be impatience. Usability expert Steve Krug, in his excellent book on web design, *Don't Make Me Think*, said "We're usually in a hurry. Much of our web use is motivated by the desire to save time." He goes on to say that most people are really only interested in a fraction of what's on a page. The reader wants information fast.

Studies show that the eyes scan quickly over the bulk of the text looking for keywords that are relevant to a need or topic of interest. People do not read word for word. In fact, they often do not read to the end of a sentence. Some studies suggest people read as few as a fifth of the words on the page, whereas others suggest a third. And they don't necessarily read in sequential order (Nielsen 2008).

There can be many reasons for this. Perhaps it is the increased cognitive effort of reading from a screen, or environmental distractions, especially when reading on a mobile device. If your learner is in a car or waiting for a plane at the airport, her brain is filtering myriad other sensory distractions. The learner could also be jumping between different tasks. It's not uncommon for web surfers to have several tabs open in their browser and skip between them, not to mention interruptions from instant messages and emails. It might simply be a symptom of modern life—people are busy and under pressure to meet many priorities.

The bottom line is that when learners read your screen text, it's likely their eyes are skipping around looking for key elements that relate to them and ignoring other parts. They are probably in a hurry, so their concentration may be less than you expect, and there may be distractions competing for their attention. The assumption that readers will start at the beginning of the sentence, read to the end, then move to the next sentence is hard to defend, as is the assumption they'll read each paragraph in order.

Visual Impact of Reading Screen Text

Reading screen text is as much a visual experience as it is linguistic. Understanding this interaction is what user experience testing and usability are all about. One of the most widely quoted experts in this field is Jakob Nielsen, who has been researching and writing about web usability since the 1990s. In 2006, Nielsen introduced the concept of the F-shaped pattern for reading. He conducted an eye-scanning study of 232 users as they surfed thousands of pages and found that when they looked at a page they first read the top line, skipped a few lines, and read across the page. They then read text more or less vertically down the left hand of the page (Figure 15-1).

Figure 15-1. F-Shaped Pattern

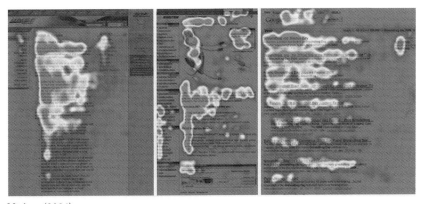

Nielsen (2006)

Think about this. Because they didn't read each line, they ended up ignoring many of the sentences someone had written. And when they did start reading a line, they didn't even read the sentence in its entirety. They read less and less as they scrolled down the page, meaning that after the introduction paragraph, their attention started to fade just as the writer was getting into the meat of the topic.

The implications are significant. Most readers will receive a largely incomplete message. Nielsen says that the eye scans a webpage at incredible speeds, which may not surprise you. For instance, you have probably had someone reply to an email asking for information that was included in your original email. They skimmed the text, but didn't read it all.

Content Below the Fold

Nielsen offers other valuable insights into readers' activities. One is related to what designers call the fold line. User experience experts refer to the bottom of the screen as the *fold*, a term borrowed from the newspaper industry. When newspapers are stacked on a newsstand, they are folded so you only see the top half of the front page. The bottom half of the page, which can't be seen on the newsstand, is referred to as "below the fold." Any content that requires you to scroll down is considered to be below the fold.

When the web was in its infancy, a lot of people did not scroll below the fold. Maybe it was a symptom of mechanics—people didn't know how to scroll or even realize that they could. In 1996, Nielsen said that having content that requires people to scroll was one of the top 10 mistakes in web design. However, he later revised his comment, finding that as time went on the percentage of web users who scroll increased (Nielsen 1997). But it doesn't necessarily mean you should start placing your most important content below the fold. While most people now scroll, Nielsen found that they spend 80 percent of their time reading content above the fold and only 20 percent below the fold (Nielsen 2010). So even though many more people scroll below the fold, most people skim over that content faster than content above the fold, making below-the-fold content less effective.

Again, consider the implications. If your summary of how to submit an electronic expense claim runs for 300 words and requires readers to scroll down the webpage, they will most likely skim over the important stuff, miss crucial points, and then have to call the help desk in frustration. If the meat of your content is in the middle of the article, there is a good chance learners will spend the least amount of time reading the important stuff.

Fonts, Justification, and Column Width

The visual elements of your page can affect how easy it is to read. One aspect is font choice. Traditionally, usability specialists recommended that webpages use sans serif fonts (Arial, Helvetica, and Verdana) because they are easier to read on the screen than serif fonts (Times New Roman). However, screen resolution has improved dramatically over the past few years and font choice may be less significant. More important, you should be consistent with font choice and avoid having too many different fonts. Also, ensure there is high contrast between the font color and the background.

The way you align your text can also affect reading. If it is right or center justified, for instance, it creates more work for the brain to search for the next line if you are used to reading from left to right; your brain has been trained to automatically swing to the left margin when you read to the end of a line. When the next line does not start at the same place as the preceding line, such as center- and right-justified text, it creates greater cognitive effort to search for the beginning of the next line.

Finding the next line is also an issue that can be affected by column width. The wider your text column, the more effort it takes to find the next line, because your eye will have moved to the right and lost its reference point at the margin. Narrow columns are thus easier to read because your eye doesn't move away from this reference point.

Linguistic Issues

It's easy to get hung up on the visual impact of web text, but solid writing is still crucial. Many of the conventions associated with Plain English can help make screen text easy to read. Plain English tends to use a less formal tone with simple words and shorter sentences. This means less scrolling and a lower cognitive load.

For example, using complex phrases such as *completing a process of elimination* instead of a simple verb such as *eliminating* just means more words to scroll through and more words to skip. *Deleting* or *cutting out* would be even better. This is important for most writing, but it is even more critical for screen text. Writing is quicker and easier to understand when sentences are short and words are familiar, delivered in a conversational tone.

In addition to following Plain English conventions, using headings and other elements can improve readability and encourage people to scroll. Presenting information in tables or bulleted lists rather than long paragraphs will make it easier for people to find the key information they are looking for.

Different Devices

Just as you should produce video viewed primarily on a smartphone differently from video viewed primarily on a television screen, you should write text for a desktop differently from text for a smartphone. This is consistent with the digital mindset from chapter 2.

It is fair to say that digital communication is still in its infancy. Although many people now rely on their phones for GPS, email, and quick access to information, the first true smartphone, the iPhone, was only released in 2007. As of this writing, that makes it younger than 10 years old. The iPad, introduced in 2010 and thus bringing tablets to the mainstream, is even younger. To be sure, developers no doubt borrowed usability wisdom learned from experiences with earlier phones such as the wireless application protocol (WAP). But smartphones have not yet made it to adolescence. It's safe to assume that mobile devices will continue to find their identity in the coming years, and as such the conventions we follow will no doubt continue to change.

But mobile usage research can help inform the way you write for smaller screens. If following Plain English conventions is important for general screen content, following even "plainer" Plain English is essential when writing text for display on mobile screens. Nielsen and Raluca Budiu, in their 2013 book, *Mobile Usability,* say that it is 108 percent harder to understand information when reading from a mobile screen. They suggest that because less information can be displayed on a screen at a time, readers must rely more on their memory of other aspects of the article. In addition to this, having to scroll takes time and diverts attention away from the content to the psychomotor skill of navigation.

When to Use Text

A central premise in this book is that you choose the modality based on what you are helping people learn. The strength in screen text lies in its ability to convey concrete information, such as legal or HR policy, scientific principles, and compliance issues. Audio and video struggle with this task, as discussed in chapters 4 and 9.

Additionally, there will be times when you need to break the multimodal rule and use text for content that would work better in a podcast or a video—not everyone has the time to record a podcast or shoot video. While this book shows you how to develop podcasts and videos fast and affordably, it can still be a lengthy process, and you might not have the necessary equipment. So it's understandable that screen text is often the default. But bear in mind that writing screen text, while quicker, also requires you to be deliberate in your approach.

Another consideration when it comes to the multimodal dynamic of screen text is how it works in tandem with podcasts, videos, and graphics. Screen text doesn't appear in a vacuum. You may plan the educational narrative to be interwoven among several modalities, playing to each one's strengths. For example, you may explain the detail with text, show the action with a video, and share other people's experiences with a podcast. In the future, this will be the ideal—to create a seamless multimodal experience—although now, as we struggle to come to grips with different modalities, we tend to see them working relatively separately.

Screen Text Work Flow

If you are reading each chapter of this book in order, you will have noticed an underlying philosophy: When you create media content of any kind, you need to be deliberate. Shooting engaging video is more than just firing up the camera and hoping for the best. Consistently engaging video requires clarity of purpose, structure, a storyboard, a script, and location planning.

Similarly, writing can seem easier than it really is. Most of us have been writing content for so long that it can feel like a simple matter of opening Microsoft Word and churning out the pages. But like video and podcasts, if you don't carefully plan your written content, it will invariably lead to screen text that is not as quick and easy to read as it can be, and the writing process will take more time.

So the plan, create, and edit process is just as important for the written word as it is for audio and video. Start with a learning objective, make sure the topic is best conveyed as screen text, break it down, and create a structure. Only when you have a skeleton structure of your writing should you pick up your pen, so to speak. For some people, writing comes naturally; for others, it can be a real struggle. But it's never not work. So be prepared to allow enough time to make sure screen text is clear, whether it's an email or instructional text embedded in an e-learning module. Remember, too, that writing is an iterative process. Very rarely will the first draft be perfect. Just take a look at the many poorly written emails clogging up your inbox. Generally, it will take two or three drafts. Producing multiple drafts is important because it helps you refine your text, remove unnecessary words, and strengthen your message.

Summary

Screen text, wherever it is, needs to be written deliberately with a focus on the intended objective. It's not something to knock out fast, but instead something that needs time and patience. It also needs to follow some new writing conventions that do not always line up with the rules of traditional grammar. And these new conventions will most likely evolve as new platforms and screens are developed.

In the following chapters, we'll explore what this means in practice. Chapter 16 looks at the new and traditional rules you need to follow to make your screen text more engaging. Chapter 17 suggests ways to review your content.

Planning and Creating Screen Text

In This Chapter

- How should you structure digital text content?
- What do you need to consider when writing your text?
- What writing tools are at your disposal?
- How do you write for beyond the webpage?

Depending on the device, screen text comes in many display shapes and sizes. Some learners will read your content on their smartphone while others will access it at their desks on their computer. The text may come in an email or tweet, be posted on a discussion board, or appear within a mobile app.

So where should you start when it comes time to plan and create screen text? Do you need a different style of writing for each device and application? In an ideal world, yes. But we don't have time to explore each and every device and how it calls for us to write for its screen. So, this chapter will focus mainly on writing digital text for the computer screen, which is still the most common screen on which learners access digital content. The initial focus will be on informational content that's 300 to 600 words, like instructional articles or blog posts. Later in the chapter we will briefly consider other screens and applications.

While writing has many complexities, it is a far more familiar process to most people than planning and creating audio or video content. So unlike the sections in this book about audio and video, the planning and creating stages of digital writing are combined into one chapter.

Planning Digital Text

Planning for how you create and edit digital content is essential. However, some content producers believe that writing is a free-flowing process and planning actually stifles creativity. Sit down, they say, and just let the ideas come to you. It's more important to be in the zone or flow than to be clear about your purpose. While this might work for literature—although I suspect it doesn't for all writers—this is not effective for factual content like learning and will slow you down. And like with podcast and video production, lack of planning makes working with a team more difficult.

The more you plan, the less you need to correct or restructure your work later in a project. It's much easier to make changes to your ideas by moving around sticky notes or bullet points before you write than picking apart a 1,000-word blog post, restructuring it, and then doing another sweep to ensure flow and consistency.

Planning starts with defining the learning objective and knowing the audience. The more focused and defined it is, the easier it will be to stay on track and keep irrelevancies from creeping into your article. Chapter 5 presented a basic overview of how to structure a learning objective and a discussion about developing personas. Once you have defined the objective and identified the persona for your learner, you'll ask the question, "What is the best modality to convey this learning?" If conveying factual details is important, such as HR policy or codes of professional conduct, text might offer the best option. The decision may not always be purely editorial. For example, video might represent the best modality for a learning objective, but you have to opt for text due to a shrinking budget. Assuming your content is ideal for digital text, you should start planning the article by creating a skeleton outline structure.

Structuring Digital Text

The more soundly you structure your content, the easier it will be to understand. Digital writers can follow numerous storytelling structures. The ROPS model, referenced in chapter 5, is easily applied to text: The first line of this model would help learners review relevant knowledge and relate the content to their needs. The inverted pyramid structure, taught to print journalists, is also a great format to follow. Jakob Nielsen recommends this structure because it provides a key summary at the top, so people who may not read everything still get the gist of it. The inverted pyramid provides the *lede,* a newspaper term journalists use to describe the first paragraph, to summarize the content in one or two sentences. Both structures feature the summary early on, positioned above the fold, where viewers' eyes first go.

People read most of the first line, skip a few lines, and read part of another line. They spend a lot of time on the left side of the page. This first sentence needs to persuade the reader that your content is valuable to minimize skimming. Consider making that first line stand out visually. Use a slightly different color from the body text or add bold to it. Or summarize the story in a few bullet points to make it quicker to read (Whitenton 2014; Schade 2015).

Nicholas Carr (2008), writing in *The Atlantic,* describes the difference between a print and digital reader. He suggests that the print reader is like a scuba diver who dives deep into the content, whereas the digital reader is like a surf skier bouncing across the waves.

The digital reader is also influenced by the visual nature of the text. Unless there are visual disruptions—and this is where the change principle comes in—the digital reader is at risk of skipping over heavy blocks of text and missing much of what you have to share. Headings and subheadings can act as disruptions. Line spaces between paragraphs can also take some of the visual cognitive weight off the page. Vary the length of paragraphs, but keep them short. Allow plenty of white space on both sides of the text column. Add relevant images, such as photographs and graphics, to disrupt the flow and draw the eye.

Creating a Skeleton Structure

A skeleton structure lists the main sections of your writing, and can be done as a bulleted list or, if you're visually inclined, a mind map. The ROPS and inverted pyramid models can act as your template. If you are using ROPS, each section could feature a level 1 heading. Then the present stage, which is longer than the other stages, could involve a series of level 2 headings, or subheadings. The inverted pyramid model starts with a lede, which might state what the learner will know or be able to do after reading the content. Then the main points of the content will be covered in order of priority.

Nonlinear Structure

In traditional media, writers had to explain the complete story in their articles. For example, if a writer was writing about managing conflict in the workplace and needed to make reference to the brain's limbic system, he would need a paragraph or two to explain it. Likewise, an article about how to change the toner on a laser printer may require an additional paragraph explaining what the drum is. This is important for folks who don't know what the limbic system is or what drums in laser photocopiers are. But it's repetitive and cumbersome for those who do.

The digital ecosystem is a nonlinear system in which content is linked and forms networks. You have the option of providing a hyperlink to another article or page that provides the background on subjects some people may not be familiar with. So instead of including two paragraphs about the limbic system or photocopier drums, you could link to an explanatory article. This enables the reader to personalize how they consume the content by giving them options not to read it as a linear story.

As you write, consider key concepts that many but not all readers may be familiar with and provide links, rather than giving some readers text they're likely to skip over. This enables people who need the information to find it and those who already have it to keep reading. This is an important part of personalizing the content.

Creating Digital Text

Once you have a skeleton outline, your structure is mostly set, with the bullets or nodes in a mind map as your headings. Now it's time to fill it in with the text. Given that people read digital text differently than printed text, it's important to follow some important conventions.

Tone

The digital ecosystem is informal, so your text should avoid formal expressions and long words. Formal writing tends to be much wordier than necessary, adding stress as the brain works to understand the message. In the end, this takes extra time for the reader.

Write one-to-one so the reader feels he is not just one person in a large audience but the only person for whom you are writing. For example, avoid, "My readers are probably aware," and instead opt for, "You are probably aware." Use of the term *we* suggests inclusivity.

Lede

As discussed earlier, the lede plays an important role in engaging your reader. It's the sentence, or sentences, that convinces the reader she'll learn by reading on. Your lede should be as short as you can make it without losing its impact; aim to keep it under 25 words. If you have more than one clause in the lede, break each one into individual sentences.

Front-load the lede so that the reader can get the gist of what he will learn even if he does not read to the end of the sentence. Let's say you're writing content for a webpage on workplace conflict. For a workbook or handout you might write, "As with any place where lots of people with varying interests interact, the workplace is a breeding ground for conflict." While this reads well in print, the key message is after the dependent clause. If your reader doesn't get to the end of the sentence, he would not know what the article was about. Instead write, "Conflict breeds easily in the workplace. It's full of people who regularly interact and have different interests." Or, "The workplace is a breeding ground for conflict. It's full of people with competing interests."

Words

It's important to choose words that are quick and easy to remember. This is where the familiarity principle kicks in. Different words can mean different things to people based on their culture, education, and personal experiences. Knowing your audience and how they use words is critical, so:

- Choose familiar words.
- Choose short words.
- Choose concrete words.
- Avoid certain pronouns.

People make sense of the world through their memories. These memories can be personal experiences or amassed knowledge. Writers also do this and can find themselves using words that relate to their own experiences and education. As a result, they use jargon and technical terms that are immediately familiar to them but not the reader. It's like the writer with an MBA who uses words like right-sizing, vertical integration, and business alignment for an audience of workers who mostly have a high-school education and don't care much for management-speak. Instead, use words that your reader will understand. Don't try to impress them with fancy words that only slow comprehension.

A common practice for media writers is to use short words. Short words are quicker to read, take less time for the brain to process, and are usually more familiar to readers.

Readers will understand your message quicker if you choose concrete words over abstract ones. Concrete words are specific and can be recognized by your senses, while abstract words are vague and cannot be tied to a sense. For example, freedom is not something you can see, smell, taste, hear, or touch. It's an intellectual construct. As are bravery and success. Abstract words are open to interpretation and do not carry as much immediate strength when conveying factual information. For example, *reached out to John* is abstract, whereas *called John* is concrete. *Bravely rescued the child* is abstract, whereas *ran through the flames to rescue the child* is concrete.

As well as going for concrete words, avoid using too many personal pronouns like *it, them,* or *they.* Instead of writing *it was on time,* use *the bus was on time.* Instead of *they reacted negatively,* use *union members reacted negatively.*

Sentences

Keeping your content short applies to sentence length as well. The shorter your sentence, the quicker it will get through the sensory register and into the working memory, where your learner can start constructing her understanding.

You can keep your sentences short in several ways:

- Write in the active voice.
- Keep each sentence to one clause.
- Delete redundant words.
- Opt for verbs rather than abstract nouns.
- Follow the "and period" rule.

The voice of your sentence refers to the order in which you place the actor and action. Sentences in the active voice put the actor before the action. For example, in the sentence, "The jazz orchestra was conducted by Felix Hassenhorp," the action is conducted. Conducted appears before the actor, Felix Hassenhorp. Thus it is written in the passive voice. If you write it in the active voice, Felix comes before the action and it would read something like, "Felix Hassenhorp [actor] conducted [action] the jazz orchestra." The active voice shortens the sentence by two words and makes it stronger. Aim to write the majority of your sentences in the active voice.

To keep your digital sentence short, limit each sentence to one clause. A clause is a single unit of meaning within a sentence. For example, the sentence, "The restaurant had closed its kitchen, but the chef still grilled a burger for the customer," has two clauses. The first is that the restaurant had closed its kitchen. The second is that the chef still grilled a burger for the customer. Sentences with two clauses take the brain longer to process. The sensory memory has to wait longer before determining whether to pass it into the working memory. Writing one clause sentences also means avoiding subordinate clauses.

Often when people first draft a sentence, they add more words than necessary. As you review a sentence, search for words you can take out that will not change its meaning. Good writers are ruthless in cutting sentences down. If you can take a word out of a sentence without substantially changing the meaning, drop it. Imagine every word is worth a few dollars; do your best to keep the cost of the sentence down.

You can reduce the length of your sentences by replacing abstract nouns with verbs. This both shortens and strengthens your sentences. "Engaging in a process of negotiation with the customer," is long and windy, whereas "negotiate with the customer" is stronger and shorter. As a general rule it's better to use verbs than nouns because they imply change, which draws people's attention.

The period plays a visual role of disruption and tells the reader to expect a new sentence. This is what I call the "and period rule," which I derive from the change principle. The more periods you have indicating change, the more the eye will be drawn to read. Often sentences are longer than they need to be because they have two clauses joined by a coordinating conjunction such as *and*. Other conjunctions include *but, or, yet,* and *so*. When you see a coordinating conjunction, consider starting a new sentence. For example, "Workplace conflict is common across most industries, and it pays to be aware of how it may affect your team" could be written, "Workplace conflict is common across most industries. It pays to be aware of how it affects your team." Sometimes you'll have a sentence with a conjunction that plays a narrative role. Consider making it the start of the next sentence. For example, "The HR department intends to introduce a new grading system for employees, but it is unlikely to be implemented this year" could be written, "The HR department intends to introduce a new grading system for employees. But it is unlikely to be implemented this year." As you read this last suggestion, you may have been thinking, "Wait a moment, I learned in grade school to never start a sentence with a preposition!" Just about any grammar expert will tell you that this rule is really a myth. You only need to look at some of the best writers to see they don't follow that rule. Most likely it was used as a set of "training wheels" to prevent us from falling into the habit of writing sentence fragments. And actually, sentence fragments work well for screen text, when people are scanning the page for keywords.

Paragraphs

Paragraphs group sentences of the same topic together in one section of text. They play a visual role in helping readers find relevant information and keep their place on the page. Aim for short paragraphs of one or two sentences. Longer ones appear as heavy blocks of text, which readers tend to skip. Make sure to separate them with a line break.

Headings

Headings play many roles in digital text. They have a navigational role in that the reader can use them to find key parts of the content. They have an editorial role in that they describe what the reader can expect to read in the paragraphs below the heading. And they have a secondary editorial role in that if your reader digests only the headings, she should get a general idea of what the article is about. They also have a visual role in breaking up the sea of body text that readers are likely to skip over.

It's tempting to adopt an almost playful tone when writing headings, as if writing for a tabloid placard. But this turns readers off. Clever turns of phrase do not work for factual content because the reader isn't reading for fun but to learn. Write headings that are descriptive and short. They should clearly explain what the reader will learn in the subsequent paragraph.

If you struggle writing headlines, start by writing a sentence that describes what the reader will discover in the paragraphs that follow the heading. Then look at the sentence and take out as many words as possible. For example:

- "How to Change a Tire on the Side of the Road" could be, "Change a Tire Roadside."
- "The Important Principle of Writing Learning Objectives" could be, "Key Principle: Write Learning Objectives."

In a print landscape, it is common to have several heading levels. However, it's good to keep digital content as simple as possible to avoid having more than a heading and subheading. Because your readers will be scrolling, they might lose track of which level they're under.

Also, adopt a capitalization policy. There are generally three ways to do this. Some capitalize the first and last word of the heading along with all principal words and any words longer than three letters. This is the AP approach and you'll see it used by the *New York Times.* The *Chicago Manual of Style* uses something similar: Capitalize the first and last word of the heading along with all pronouns, nouns, verbs, adverbs, adjectives, and subordinating conjunctions. The second approach is to capitalize just the first word and any proper nouns. This is how the *L.A. Times* writes its headlines. The third approach is to capitalize all words in the heading. Which is best? There are varying viewpoints on this and the choice you make is probably less important than being consistent and sticking to one style.

Another issue for headings is whether to finish a heading with a period. From a visual perspective, it's probably best not to use a period because it's just another visual element for the sensory register to process. But again, it's more important to consistently do one or the other.

Lists

Construct a list when you need to describe a number of connected items. It will be easier for your reader if the items are not all in one sentence. When these items need to be considered consecutively, such as steps to take when logging into a computer, you can use a numerical list. When there is no order or priority, you can use bullets.

For example, rather than writing, "When planning a meeting, make sure you create an agenda, invite participants, book the meeting room, and assign a note taker," you could construct it as:

When planning a meeting:

- Create an agenda.
- Invite participants.
- Book the meeting room.
- Assign a note taker.

It's important to construct your lists following a parallel structure. In the example above, notice each bullet started with a verb.

Captions

As readers scan your written text, their eyes are drawn to elements that stand out. Captions, when attached to images or graphics, are one disruptive element that can draw eyeballs. When you write a caption, front-load the message so people can get the gist of it without reading to the end.

Captions play a valuable role when they add to the image. Avoid explaining what is obvious in the image—allow the picture to speak for itself. If you have a photograph of someone typing on a laptop, don't write the caption, "Pedro Gonzalez writes on his laptop." It's obvious what he's doing. Instead explain why he is typing or why it is important. For example, "Upload your expenses using the portal and you'll be reimbursed within 10 business days." Or, "Your expenses will be reimbursed within 10 business days when you upload them using the portal."

Writing Tools

Most people are likely to write their learning content in a word processor such as Microsoft Word. Today's word processors have incredible power and support the writer with styles, references, and review tools such as spelling and grammar checks.

However, despite all that word processors have to offer, most are designed for business applications rather than writing. Writers need to juggle tasks such as structuring content, accessing and managing research notes, compiling graphics, and keeping notes on their project.

Tools are available today to help writers with these tasks, such as Scrivener, Storyist, yWriter5, and WriteItNow. These software programs help you organize your thoughts, view your research or notes side-by-side with multiple screens, and manage your ideas using virtual index cards, storyboards, and setting sheets. While these are mostly designed for book authors they are still excellent tools for managing multiple pieces of text content.

Digital text is displayed on screens using hypertext markup language (HTML), a set of tags that precede your words and tell your browser how to display a piece of text (Figure 16-1). For example, to display a word in bold, you would add the HTML tag <bold> before the actual word and </bold> after it. HTML also tells the browser how to display nontext content, such as audio and video, and gives it instructions on how to lay out the page. HTML5, the current standard determined by the World Wide Web Consortium, takes HTML into the realm where playing audio, video, and animated content like Flash is much more practical.

Figure 16-1. Example of Code From a Web Browser

```
4652
4653
4654   <h1>
4655       Rapid Video Development for Trainers
4656   </h1>
4657
4658   <h2 class="authorname">By
4659       <a href="#authors">
4660            <span id="maincontent_0_Authors" class="authorblue">Jonathan Halls</span></a></h2>
4661
4662
4663       <div class="samplechapter">
4664           <div class="chapterlft">
4665               <img src="/common/img/pdf-icon1.gif"><a class="chapertink" href="http://files.astd.org/Publication-Attachments/111215/Sample?
free chapter of this book
4666                   </a>
4667           </div>
4668           <div class="chapterrht">
4669           </div>
4670           <div class="clear"></div>
4671       </div>
4672
4673
4674
4675   <div class="fl_left margin_r publication-image">
4676       <img src="https://d2p9xuzeb0m4p4.cloudfront.net/~/media/Images/Publications/Publication-Covers/111215_Rapid_Video_Development_for_Tr?
h=184&amp;la=en&amp;w=150&amp;hash=3472680E7E20C7FEB8EC65EDB8DB48BDA1247FAA" class="gray-border" alt="111215 Rapid Video Development for
4677   </div>
4678   <div class="introtxt">
4679       <span id="maincontent_0_Description"><p><strong><a href="http://files.astd.org/Publication-Attachments/111215/Sample%20Chapter%208.p?
Video</a></strong></p>
4680   <p><a href="/Publications/Books/Rapid-Video-Development-for-Trainers/Rapid-Video-Development-for-Trainers-Videos" shape="rect"><strong>V:
   </a></p><div class='read-more-content'>
4681   <p><em>Rapid Video Development for Trainers</em> meets the needs of companies and individuals who are thinking about or have dabbled in ?
focused, high quality video is well within the capability of nearly every development professional, the skill sets required to do so have
trainers&rsquo; job descriptions. This is where <em>Rapid Video Development</em> <em>for Trainers</em> comes in: a comprehensive tutoria?
video development, this book provides both the theoretical overview and the nuts-and-bolts instructions for creating professional quality
inexpensively. </p>
```

In the early days of the web, writers and web designers coded their own digital text. They did this in web editing software programs such as Dreamweaver or Homesite. However, as technology developed, programs like Microsoft FrontPage offered web writers the option of automatically writing code, so instead of having to insert <bold> before a word you simply needed to select the word and click on bold, as you would in a word processor.

These programs provided loads of control over website design—probably more than many digital writers wanted. So along came content management systems (CMSs), which had set templates. Writers would write their text, drop it into a window in the software along with any images or video links, and it would be automatically published. Large corporations bought specific content management systems, whereas small businesses and writers started using the popular and accessible CMS WordPress, which started out as a blog management platform. WordPress is behind millions of websites around the world. Other CMSs include Drupal and Joomla. As the web grows in complexity, CMSs take a lot of the hard work out of managing web publishing so writers can focus on text and other modalities such as graphics. One advantage is that CMSs will automatically generate the content to work for multiple platforms through responsive design techniques. They also add search engine optimization options.

Learning management systems are like CMSs except they are geared for learning and do things like track attendance and completion of online learning. Most learning professionals will create digital text in word processors and drop them into learning management systems.

Digital Text Beyond the Web Screen

The conventions covered so far have been mostly focused on writing digital text for the computer screen, on the Internet, or on your company's intranet. However, the principles also apply to email, mobile content, and posting commentary in learning management systems such as discussion boards. While they all follow the same principles, let's touch on some specifics.

Email

Learning professionals use email to share nanolearning and instructions related to learning events. Make sure the subject line is descriptive and short (Figure 16-2). Front-load your message so the first few words tell the learners what the email is about. Make sure the first sentence within the email provides a good summary and an explanation either of what they are learning or what they need to do. Put a line space between each sentence so each one stands out. Use bullets for related information. If your email is long, make sure to use headings and consider making those headings a different but similar color to the body text. Use short, one-clause sentences. It's important to be even more ruthless in removing unnecessary words from your sentences because of how quickly people read email.

Figure 16-2. Examples of a Good and Bad Email

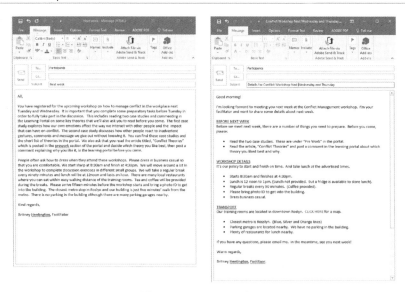

People reading the email on the left are likely to skip most of the content because it's a heavy block of text. However, the email on the right allows easier scanning through the use of bulleted lists, headings, and more white space.

Mobile Platforms

People view mobile content with more impatience than traditional computer screens. So keep anything meant for a mobile screen short, especially for smartphones (Figure 16-3). Use images when you can. The screen is small and fonts appear even smaller. Use lots of bulleted lists and keep paragraphs very short so your text does not appear as heavy blocks of text. A short paragraph on a desktop computer looks like a very long block of text on a smartphone. Smartphone text should be half the length of content on a desktop computer.

Figure 16-3. Text on Desktop and Mobile Screens

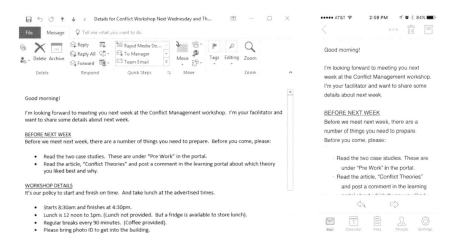

The same content can look very different on a desktop (left) and a smartphone (right).

Summary

Digital text is used in many ways. It's read on the screens of desktop and laptop computers, smartphones, and tablets. And it's used in online articles, lesson plans, workshop materials, emails, and discussion boards. Learners do not read digital text word for word; instead, they skip around the page looking for keywords. When crafting digital text, you cannot write with the assumption that learners will read a whole sentence or paragraph, as with print matter. The key to digital writing is to remove any word that's not necessary. Keep everything short and structure your content so readers know at the top of the page what they're going to learn. In today's fast-paced environment, where mobile users are continually jumping between apps to consume text messages, social media posts, and games, you need to ensure that your digital text achieves its goal of delivering learning.

Editing Screen Text for Learning

In This Chapter

- What is the purpose of editing?
- How do you conduct a substantive edit or a copy edit?
- What is the most efficient process of editing?

Editing text is different from editing in audio and video production. When digital text is ready for editing, the words have already been assembled in order and the sequence or flow is more or less satisfactory. What is required at this point is a review to ensure the content is accurate, the structure flows logically in a way that makes sense to the reader, words are spelled correctly, and nontext elements like audio, video, and graphics function correctly.

In many learning departments, the task of editing often falls to the person on the team who has a good eye for detail or just likes grammar. This person usually has an instinctive set of skills that keeps you out of trouble. However, editing is a professional process that follows its own work flow, and these skills can be learned with practice. In different fields, the work flow may have slightly different nuances, but it is always consistent. A newspaper copy editor will have a different take from a technical editor who works on instructional manuals, while a book editor will come from yet a different perspective.

If editing is not your primary occupation, as it most likely is not for the learning professional, you just want your final text to be accurate, easy to read, and functional for the reader. So you're probably less inclined to care which methodology to follow. For that reason, we're going to be less concerned about a standard approach to editing digital text than with what you need to consider as you check your own or someone else's content.

When you have created your text, you need to check the substance of the content and its correctness. The substance refers to the accuracy of the content, its structure, and the construction of individual paragraphs and sentences. This is an analytical task that requires editorial judgment. The correctness is making sure words are spelled correctly and everything on the page works. This is a more methodical task that requires you to check the way text has been written against rules of usage and corporate style guides. Aspects of these two stages overlap, but it is handy to see them separately to ensure you remain focused when you edit.

This chapter will run through these in more detail. While these steps relate to digital text, whether it be a PowerPoint slide, an email, or a discussion board, the examples will be based on a learning article, such as a blog post or piece of instructional content in a learning management system.

Conducting a Substantive Edit

When conducting a substantive edit, you need to check your content's accuracy, macrostructure, and microstructure.

Accuracy

At this stage, don't worry about checking for spelling mistakes or grammar. Your text may change many times and spending time correcting words that may not even end up in your final article is a waste of time. Instead, read through the article and check all the facts. This could include names of people mentioned, dates and times of events, names of brands and locations, and names of theories. Check that what is said is correct. For example, if you are writing about "I statements" in an article on conflict resolution, make sure the article is consistent with best practice by checking other sources. If sources are being quoted, check these too. If you are a subject matter expert, you may not need to conduct research on these facts because you know them well. But if in doubt, check it.

You can conduct an accuracy edit by simply reading through the article, writing down any facts or assumptions that need to be checked on a separate piece of paper, then going and checking them in turn. If you wrote the article yourself, it could be a good idea to have a subject matter expert check it over for you.

Macrostructure

When you are happy with the accuracy of your content, you should review how it flows. Remember, the purpose of text editing is to make the ideas you are writing about quicker and easier to understand for your learner. So keep in mind how your reader is likely to see the content. Think about what experiences she may use to make sense of it.

Read through the article and note the major sections. Don't get bogged down in the detail; this is about getting a sense of the overall flow. Does each section flow from one to the next in a logical order? If you're writing about how to make a cup of coffee, do you explain the steps in a way that will make sense for the reader? This is a process of analysis for which you must exercise editorial judgment because there is probably no right or wrong answer, just a better or worse answer.

Does the article have a strong introduction that gives the reader the "what's in it for me?" rationale? Does it have a strong summary? Are the headings positioned at the key stages of the article to develop the ideas? How about analogies being used—are they familiar enough to make sense for the learner? How about the links—are words or phrases in the article that may not be familiar to readers linked to other articles that will shed light on them? And do you have multimodal content such as audio, video, or graphics positioned at appropriate points in the article? Are they the best pieces of content for the narrative or can you recommend better ones? Also, do you have permission to use them? Make sure you have licenses or release forms.

Microstructure

When you are satisfied that the sections of the article are blocked together in a way that's quick and easy to understand, it's time to review the microstructure. Some folks are inclined to review both the macro- and microstructures at the same time, but it can be helpful to treat these as separate tasks.

The task of reviewing microstructure is less about how the ideas block together and more about how clear the building blocks are. It's about making sure paragraphs, sentences, headings, and other elements quickly make sense to the reader.

As mentioned, people read digital text differently from printed text, so you need to look for different elements. You also need to maintain a visual sense of how the article appears on the screen the learner uses.

Make sure paragraphs contain one idea and are short, preferably two sentences. This may mean breaking up a long paragraph into several. Check that sentences front-load their message, consist of one clause, and are written mostly in the active voice. Replace abstract nouns with verbs and make sure the words are concrete. Review each word in each sentence to be sure it's necessary, removing it if it's not. And look at lists to be sure they are constructed in parallel phrases.

Checking clarity extends to other textual elements such as headings, captions, and hyperlinks. Headings should be written in parallel—for example, if three of your four headings are written as nouns and the fourth is a phrase, you should adjust the fourth to a noun. Captions should be front-loaded and add new information that is not obvious in the picture. To ensure consistency, it is easier to review all headings at once, all captions at once, all links at once, and so forth.

Remember to review word choice based on your audience, and be sure the tone is informal. Complex words should be replaced with simple words that are quick and easy to recognize. Make sure the text is consistently in first, second, or third person.

Once the substantive edit has been finished, the article should be in good shape. It will be accurate, flow easily for the reader in a logical way, and the actual words, sentences, paragraphs, and other supporting elements will be clear and consistent. Now it's time to check that everything is correct.

Conducting a Copy Edit

In the newspaper world, the copy editor is the last person to check an article. She will read through and make sure the spelling is correct and everything is in good grammatical shape. There's little point worrying about this review until you have conducted the substantive edit, simply because you may find yourself correcting sentences or even paragraphs that end up on the proverbial chopping block.

At the copy edit stage, you need to be disciplined and not make substantial changes to the text. It's a good idea to adopt a style guide for editing. You could use the *Chicago Manual of Style* or develop your own. The key to making your content professional is to be consistent with how you present your information. Here are a few things to look out for as you engage in the copy edit.

First, make sure all the words are spelled correctly. You can use spell-check on a word processor for this at a first glance, but don't rely on it. Do a check yourself to be sure words like there, their, or they're are used properly. Check that peoples' names are spelled correctly, along with locations, brand names, and technical terms. Don't forget to check captions and hyperlinks, which may be outside the body text.

Second, check for grammar and punctuation. You will be less constrained by traditional grammar for digital text than for simple punctuation. If you have periods after headings and bullets (although this is not recommended), make sure they come after all of them. Be consistent in the way you use bullets and dashes.

Check that all the links in the article work. This is a detail-orientated task that takes time, but doing it before you publish to the learning management system is easier than fielding emails about broken links. If your page is up for a while, create a document that lists all the links and put it on your calendar to check whether they're still live in three months' time.

Examine the images you are using. Do they have alt tags? Alt tags are short pieces of text that describe an image. In certain browsers such as Internet Explorer, when you roll your mouse over an image this text will pop up. Alt tags were designed for viewing web documents without images and for people who use screen readers, which cannot describe a picture. These are important for accessibility. Also check that the images have been optimized for the web. Original images such as photos are usually very large file sizes because they have high resolutions. Optimizing an image is the process of compressing the file size so it downloads quickly. (Many learning management systems do this for you but if yours doesn't, double-check your images.) While checking for optimized images is not strictly about text, it's still an important review while editing.

Check any videos you are embedding in the article. First, make sure they work. If you are embedding a video from a site like YouTube that someone else has produced and maintains, put a note on your calendar to check periodically that they haven't changed it or taken it down. Test the video from your site. If the video is something you have created and uploaded, see how it looks when you play it within your page, and adjust the settings so it plays the way you want. For example, in Vimeo you can adjust settings that automatically load another related video after the first one has stopped playing or have it simply start again. What do you want? Be consistent with your videos so they all follow the same settings. Also, some video sites will give you the option to take their logos off the video. All are elements worth considering.

Finally, look at how the page will be viewed by the reader. Check the display in multiple browsers. If your content will be viewed mostly by people on a cell phone, review it on a cell phone to make sure the formatting works.

The Process of Editing

One of the biggest obstacles to editing is being too close to your text. Because you're familiar with it, it's easy to skip over words that would normally stand out. So create some distance between you and the text. Take a break after writing so you can approach the text with a fresh mind. If time permits, edit it the next day.

It also helps to have someone else review your text for you. If you get someone else, be clear about what you want them to do. If you want a substantive edit, be clear you're not interested in typos and grammar. If it's a copy edit, tell them you're not changing the article. That way they are focused and won't give you feedback you don't want.

It's a good idea to print your text out and edit off paper. This helps create distance because it's physically and visually different from the screen. You can also more easily mark the page, unless you're working in some word processing software. Some people insist they're fine editing off a screen but to me paper is more deliberate and slows you down, reducing distractions from email or other applications.

Editing requires a lot of concentration, so do it in short bursts. While editing a single article is not going to be an all-day task, you may be tasked with reviewing 20 articles, blog posts, or pieces of digital content. If you do them all in one sitting, you'll find your energy and concentration is difficult to sustain.

Editing is also a solo task, so make sure to work where you won't have distractions such as other people or media devices. It's impossible to give your text full attention if you have a radio or television in the background that fights for space in your working memory and increases the load on your sensory memory. Some people argue they can and do so admirably, but if they did not have these distractions their concentration would be better and they'd work faster.

There are many old tricks that editors use that you may find useful. Some editors will read backwards from the last word to the first so that they consider each word on its own. That way they are not distracted by the sentence structure or other things as they read. Others will take a piece of paper and read from the top, but cover all the words below the line they are currently reading so they don't get distracted.

Don't attempt to achieve all your editing tasks in one read-through. Your brain wasn't designed like that. Allow yourself the time to do several read-throughs. Start with the substantive edit. Check the accuracy, then the structure, then the microstructure. After these three read-throughs, move on to the copy edit. When you do the copy edit, check all the headings at once. All the links at once. All the captions. It will be easier on your brain to pick up things that go wrong and ensure consistency.

Summary

The purpose of editing is making your text quicker and easier for your reader to understand. Editors from different traditions will debate certain ways to approach the edit, but what's most important is that you make sure the content is accurate and easy to read. The approaches in this chapter can become a start for your own approach and will help you avoid any major problems.

However, there is one thing worth noting. Just about every newspaper, book publisher, and e-learning publisher has paid scrupulous attention to editing and then, after the content has been published, discovered a typo. It's going to happen, so don't beat yourself up if you miss something. Just make sure you fix it and remember that we're all human.

References

Atkinson, R.C., and R.M. Shiffrin. 1968. "Human Memory: A Proposed System and Its Control Processes." In *The Psychology of Learning and Motivation*, vol. 2, edited by K. Spence and J. Spence, 89-195. New York: Academic Press.

Baddeley, A.D. 1999. *Essentials of Human Memory*. East Sussex, UK: Psychology Press Limited.

Big Black Dog Communications. 2016. "The School of the Air and Remote Learning." Australian Government, January 18. www.australia.gov.au/about-australia/australian-story/school-of-the-air.

Booker, C. 2004. *The Seven Basic Plots*. London: Continuum.

Carr, N. "Is Google Making Us Stupid?" *The Atlantic*, July/August. www.theatlantic.com/magazine/archive/2008/07/is-google-making-us-stupid/306868.

Cowan, N. 2001. "The Magical Number 4 in Short-Term Memory: A Reconsideration of Mental Storage Capacity." *The Behavioral and Brain Science* 24: 87-114.

Cron, L. 2012. *Wired for Story*. Berkeley, CA: Ten Speed Press.

Das, J.K. 2007. "Educational Broadcast Through Radio." *Journal of All India Association for Educational Research* 19(1-2). www.aiaer.net/ejournal/vol19107/8.htm.

Dreier, T. 2016. "Video Will Make Up 70% of Mobile Traffic by 2021, Says Ericsson." Streaming Media, June 1. www.streamingmedia.com/Articles/News/Online-Video-News/Video-Will-Make-Up-70-of-Mobile-Traffic-by-2021-Says-Ericsson-111441.aspx.

Follett, A. 2015. "18 Big Video Marketing Statistics and What They Mean for Your Business." Video Brewery. www.videobrewery.com/blog/18-video-marketing-statistics.

IDC (International Data Corporation). 2013. *Always Connected: How Smartphones and Social Keep Us Engaged*. Framingham, MA: IDC Research. www.academia.edu/7042070/Always_Connected_How_Smartphones_And_Social_Keep_Us_Engaged.

Krug, S. 2000. *Don't Make Me Think*. San Francisco: New Riders Publishing.

Mager, R.F. 1962. *Preparing Objectives for Programmed Instruction*. Belmont, CA: Fearon.

Malamed, C. 2011. *Visual Language for Designers.* Beverly, MA: Rockport Publishers.

McKee, R. 1997. *Story.* New York: HarperCollins.

Miller, G.A. 1956. "The Magical Number Seven, Plus or Minus Two: Some Limits on Our Capacity for Processing Information." *Psychological Review* 63(2): 81-97.

Murch, W. 2001. *In the Blink of an Eye.* Los Angeles: Silman James Press.

Newport, F. 2015. "Most U.S. Smartphone Owners Check Phone at Least Hourly." *Gallup,* July 9. www.gallup.com/poll/184046/smartphone-owners-check-phone-least-hourly.aspx.

Nielsen, J. 1996. "Original Top 10 Mistakes in Web Design." Nielsen Normal Group, May 1. www.nngroup.com/articles/original-top-ten-mistakes-in-web-design.

———. 1997. "Changes in Web Usability Since 1994." Nielsen Norman Group, December 1. www.nngroup.com/articles/changes-in-web-usability-since-1994.

———. 2006. "F-Shaped Pattern for Reading Web Content." Nielsen Normal Group, April 17. www.nngroup.com/articles/f-shaped-pattern-reading-web-content.

———. 2008. "How Little Do Users Read?" Nielsen Norman Group, May 6. www.nngroup.com/articles/how-little-do-users-read.

———. 2010. "Scrolling and Attention." Nielsen Norman Group, March 22. www.nngroup.com/articles/scrolling-and-attention.

Nielsen, J., and R. Budiu. 2013. *Mobile Usability.* Berkeley, CA: New Riders.

Schade, A. 2015. "The Fold Manifesto: Why the Page Fold Still Matters." Nielsen Norman Group, February 1. www.nngroup.com/articles/page-fold-manifesto.

Sperling, G. 1960. "The Information Available in Brief Visual Presentations." *Psychological Monographs: General and Applied* 74(11): 1-29.

Sweller, J. 1988. "Cognitive Load During Problem Solving: Effects on Learning." *Cognitive Science* 12(2): 257-285.

UNESCO. n.d. "Technologies in Support of Education." UNESCO. www.unesco.org/education/educprog/50y/brochure/promotin/194.htm.

Visible Measures. 2010. "Benchmarking Viewer Abandonment in Online Video." Visible Measures, September 29. www.visiblemeasures.com/2010/09/29/benchmarking-viewer-abandonment-in-online-video.

Whitenton, K. 2014. "Satisficing: Quickly Meet Users' Main Needs." Nielsen Norman Group, March 30. www.nngroup.com/articles/satisficing.

About the Author

 Jonathan Halls helps trainers and talent professionals learn professional media skills to create engaging learning content while supporting training executives who want their teams to become digital content factories. With a foot in both the learning and media worlds, he has taught media for more than 25 years in 30 countries. Today, Jonathan provides workshops, webinars, coaching, and consulting in most aspects of content creation, production, and work flow. He also speaks and teaches on organizational leadership, change, communication, innovation, and learning (train-the-trainer programs). Based in Washington, D.C., he is also an adjunct professor at the George Washington University, where he teaches digital media in a master's program.

Jonathan started his career in radio and has worked as a journalist, talk show host, and assistant radio station manager. Before moving to the United States, he was a learning executive at the BBC in London, where he led its prestigious production training department, which delivered the corporation's television, radio operations, new media, and safety training. Jonathan sees himself as a media generalist and has worked across radio, television, and print. He still runs workshops for print media professionals and broadcasters around the globe, including in London, Frankfurt, Paris, Dubai, Singapore, Malaysia, India, and Myanmar. He has worked for brands including the *Financial Times*, the *Daily Telegraph*, and ITV. Jonathan also served on the jury for WAN-IFRA's prestigious European Digital Media Awards, Middle East Digital Media Awards, and Asian Digital Media Awards.

Jonathan is author of *Rapid Video Development for Trainers* and *Video Script Writing*. He is a contributing author to the *ASTD Handbook: The Definitive Reference for Training & Development* and *Speak More*. His articles have been published in *TD*, *Stage Screen and Radio*, and the *HR Observer*. He has bachelor's and master's degrees in adult learning and is passionate about learning and cognition.

Jonathan is actively involved in the talent development profession. He was the founding president of ATD's UK Global Network and has served on the education committees for the ATD International Conference & Exposition and TechKnowledge. He was also on the jury for the ATD BEST Awards. He regularly speaks at many ATD chapters around the United States as well as various conferences around the world.

Follow Jonathan's nanolearning modules on creating engaging learning content at www.RapidMediaForLearning.com.

Index

In this index, *f* denotes figure and *t* denotes table.

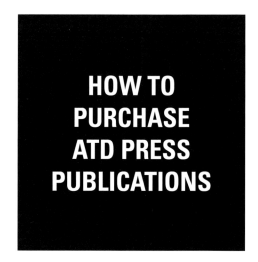

HOW TO PURCHASE ATD PRESS PUBLICATIONS

ATD Press publications are available worldwide in print and electronic format.

To place an order, please visit our online store: www.td.org/books.

Our publications are also available at select online and brick-and-mortar retailers.

Outside the United States, English-language ATD Press titles may be purchased through the following distributors:

United Kingdom, Continental Europe, the Middle East, North Africa, Central Asia, Australia, New Zealand, and Latin America
Eurospan Group
Phone: 44.1767.604.972
Fax: 44.1767.601.640
Email: eurospan@turpin-distribution.com
Website: www.eurospanbookstore.com

Asia
Cengage Learning Asia Pte. Ltd.
Phone: (65)6410-1200
Email: asia.info@cengage.com
Website: www.cengageasia.com

Nigeria
Paradise Bookshops
Phone: 08033075133
Email: paradisebookshops@gmail.com
Website: www.paradisebookshops.com

South Africa
Knowledge Resources
Phone: +27 (11) 706.6009
Fax: +27 (11) 706.1127
Email: sharon@knowres.co.za
Web: www.kr.co.za

For all other territories, customers may place their orders at the ATD online store: **www.td.org/books**.

021545.62220